What others are saying about

Dr. Gayla Holley and
Growing the Leader Within You

I was delighted to learn of your outstanding work on behalf of your community. Your generosity and willingness to serve others merit the highest praise. We must not allow ourselves to be measured by the sum of our possessions or the size of our bank accounts. The true measure of any individual is found in the way he or she treats others—and the person who regards others with love, respect, and charity holds a priceless treasure in his heart. With that in mind I have often noted that from now on in America any definition of a successful life must include serving others. Your efforts provide a shining example of this standard. Barbara joins in congratulating you and in sending you our warm best wishes for the future. May God bless you always.

President George H. W. Bush, The United States of America

I urge you to continue your important work and to encourage those around you to engage with you in serving the community. Your work and personal commitment to direct and consequential voluntary service is critical to America's future.

C. Gregg Petersmeyer, Assistant to the President
Director, Office of National Service

My prayers are with you. Thank you for opening your doors to so many in need.

Amy Blanchett, Field Representative,
Congressman Ted Poe,
Congress of the United States, House of Representatives

Your activities and selfless giving of your time and talent are most admirable and deserving of recognition. The late Walt Disney also felt strongly about contributions to the community. He once said that, "The greatest moments in life are not concerned with selfish achievements, but rather with the things we do for the people."

Michael Eisner, Chairman, The Walt Disney Company

I am proud of the support you have provided to those in need, financially and emotionally. You are a credit to the community you serve.

Jim Edgar, Governor, Illinois

In recognition of her dedication and efforts to provide a community service, the Houston Police Department of Houston, Texas is proud to present the Humanitarian Service Award to Dr. Gayla Holley. This Award is given for your dedication and voluntary service to enhance the lives of citizens and create good-will on behalf of the Houston Police Department.

Charles A. McClelland. Jr., Chief of Police, Houston, Texas

My mom was the one in our house who made things happen. She could see a need in the community, family, neighbors, church, and immediately come up with a plan to solve the problem.

Mom Gayla reminds me of her…. She will "bug" people *sweetly* to make them aware of the problem and her solutions and *give* them *the privilege to help*.

Since she was raised in the jungles of Africa in a bush pilot family, Dr. Gayla has seen poverty that none of you will ever see. That is why she is so passionate, caring, demanding…the General of the Forces surrounding her whom she leads to the great disasters of the world. You should see her in her boots, wading through the mud to give milk to hungry babies and hold them in her arms, give diapers to the mothers, give clothes for the little naked ones….

You cannot go…but she is willing *to go for you*…if we all surround her with love and resources.

You must read her story…there is nothing like it. Read what her three brothers say about her passion for the HUNGRY children. For fifty-plus years I have been in humanitarian work in major disasters around the world—twenty-five orphanages, five leper colonies, a jungle hospital in Bangladesh and a school in Thailand. Dr. Gayla is an inspiration to me and the hundreds who work with her. You will never again read a book like this one….

Lonnie Rex, B. Mus., D.D., H.L.D., K.M., L.L.D.,
Knighted in Moscow, Russia for World Humanitarian Work,
Founder of The David Livingston Foundation

Your commitment and dedication to the spirit of volunteerism in our great nation is truly commendable. Please accept my best wishes for your continued success.

Robert C. Goizueta, Chairman and Chief Executive Officer,

The Coca-Cola Company

Gayla, we appreciate your partnership in our community. Looking forward to more!

Debra Brooks Feazelle, City Manager, LaPorte, Texas

This wonderful book *Growing the Leader Within You*—by my amazing sister—is sure to inspire every reader, as you discover how life is lived and important lessons are learned in other parts of the world. Laughing and perhaps crying while journeying through this collection of unforgettable stories, everyone exploring its contents will be encouraged while living out his or her own story.

Alan Latta, Senior Pastor www.alanlatta.blogspot.com

Generations Church of Granbury www.generationspeople.org

Member of the Lake Granbury Ministerial Alliance

Antioch Oasis International, an Apostolic Leadership Network

Growing the Leader Within You is life-changing! It will show you how to overcome any challenge you face. It's practical, real, and useful for everyday life. You won't be able to set this book down once you start reading it! My sister is the storyteller of the family and her words help you to see exactly how life is around the world. From cover to cover, these principles work for leaders!

Marvin Latta

Founder of Particular Peoples Painter Co

www.particularpeoplespainter.com

Founder of StreetReach marvinlattasmusic.yolasite.com

Songwriter: Project Timeless Soul, Transparent Heart

Through the years, I have watched my sister with incredible awe. This woman has fed thousands, taught thousands, clothed thousands, and given of herself selflessly. Her genuine concern and attention to detail is unparalleled. No one is unimportant to her. I do not know of another person whose passion for others is as effective. I have always believed there are good decisions and there are bad decisions, but indecision is what makes people crazy. Decision making is the hallmark of good leadership. To be decisive, one must conquer one's fear of pain. Growing up with my sister, it became obvious early on that she had no fear of pain. She has fearlessly embarked on numerous ventures that were not for the fearful or the faint of heart. Yet she was decisive, resolute, and driven. I respect her courage and determination in the face of overwhelming odds. My sister, the fearless decision maker. *Growing the Leader Within You* is genuine, strong, and full of wise advice. You will love it!

Regan Latta, L.U.T.C.F., Farmers Insurance Agent

www.farmersagent.com/rlatta

Four Toppers Club Awards, The Blue Vase Award

The Blue Max Award, Farmers Insurance Walk of Fame,

Texas Monthly "Five Star" Agent

I enjoyed so much visiting with your mom and dad at the VFMA. Then I received a letter from your mom concerning the wonderful project you have started. The Lord bless you and your husband for such a worthy program. I enjoyed all of you so much in Liberia. What wonderful memories. God is so good.

Missionary Else Lund, Liberia, Ghana, Nigeria, Senegal, Ivory Coast,

Togo, Kenya, Tanzania, Uganda, Scotland, Denmark

I have great appreciation for Gayla's life and service and do give recognition of her works as a humanitarian, scholar, theologian, pastor, missionary, and teacher.

Dr. Donald Ned Hicks, Chancellor, American Bible College

Senior Bishop, Independent Christian Churches International

Growing the Leader Within You will raise your self-awareness, pique your curiosity and inspire you to take the action steps to transform your life. This book offers keys to unlock the doors to your most heartfelt dreams and aspirations."

Susan Friedmann, CSP, international best selling author of

Riches in Niches: How to Make it BIG in a small Market

A Blueprint to Become the Visionary Our World Desperately Needs

GROWING THE LEADER WITHIN YOU

LEVERAGING ADVERSITY INTO YOUR SUCCESS IN LIFE, WORK, LEADERSHIP AND FAITH

apr 2013

Mom —
Here's your
Success in
every part of
life! Much love
Brenda

AVIVA
PUBLISHING
NEW YORK

DR. GAYLA HOLLEY
Founder of MomsAgainstHunger.org

GROWING THE LEADER WITHIN YOU

Published by:
Aviva Publishing
Lake Placid, NY
518-523-1320
www.avivapubs.com

Please address all inquiries to:

Address all inquiries to: Dr Gayla Holley

Moms Against Hunger

2104 Underwood

LaPorte TX 77571
www.MomsAgainstHunger.org
www.GrowingTheLeaderWithinYou.com

Print ISBN: 978-1-938686-45-0

Library of Congress Control Number: 2013903998

Editor: Tyler Tichelaar

Book Cover Design: Francesco Benvenuto

Interior Book Layout: Fusion Creative Works, www.fusioncw.com

For additional copies please visit:
www.GrowingTheLeaderWithinYou.com

Foreword

by Kevin Allen

Growing up with great parents, I was taught the real meaning of life. They taught me that the most important things in this world are faith, family, and service. My father was an amazing man who displayed many leadership skills I would try all my life to develop and pass on to my own children.

As I grew up and experienced my own adventures in business, always trying to be honorable and true to my ideals, I found a need for direction at every level and at every walk of life. I could not help but wonder why some people are successful and some people are not. This question plagued me for years as I began to pursue a career as an entrepreneur until I finally discovered the answer.

What I discovered was that successful people developed a sense of community, a sense of giving back to others in need. These people have developed leadership skills that taught them that life is not just about making lots of money and living the American Dream. Rather, it is about empowering others, always offering a hand up to help guide those in need, and assisting others in achieving their dreams.

I learned that real leaders spend very little time soaking in the spotlight, but they spend most of their time helping others develop their leadership skills so they too can maximize their potential.

Almost all successful people are leaders; they have a burning desire to succeed, and they will do anything and everything to serve others, mentor others, and help others achieve their goals. In doing so, these leaders achieve their own goals as a side benefit to a life committed to service. It was Zig Ziglar who said: "You can have everything in life you want as long as you are willing to help enough other people get what they want." To me there are no such people as leaders without others close behind in their wake.

In this incredible book by Dr. Gayla Holley, you will learn that you too have this incredible leader within you, only waiting for you to unleash its direction, power, and guidance for your life. You will learn the importance of leveraging your leadership skills not only to achieve success, but more importantly, to become a humanitarian, giving of your time, your passion, and your money to assist the less fortunate of this world. You will learn that faith, family, and service to others are the most important attributes to leaving a real legacy for others to follow.

In *Growing the Leader Within You*, Dr. Holley offers you a blueprint you can follow to help you step outside of your box, expand your comfort zone, and build a business that benefits and serves others. This road map will help you identify what is truly important in life and set you on a track to be a giver of love in all areas of your life. Such a life is foreordained to bring the highest returns in physical as well as spiritual rewards.

When you follow the strategies, techniques, and ideas offered in this book, you will learn that you have a greater purpose for your life, a calling, a mission that you can begin to comprehend and then you can prepare for a life of service, be it in your own community or on the other side of the globe.

You will find yourself on the edge of your seat, cheering for Dr. Gayla as she tells her personal stories of living deep in the jungle in an African village in Liberia, West Africa. Her stories of wild animals, plane crashes, and being held at gunpoint at a border crossing with a three-month-old daughter in her arms are just a few of her many experiences that will teach you lessons you will find nowhere else.

You will learn of her real-life leadership put into action as she mentors small business owners and enterprises in Guatemala to help the local people become entrepreneurs and provide for themselves and their families. Her adventures around the world serving people in need will inspire you. You will learn how Dr. Gayla founded **MomsAgainstHunger.org** and how she has taken it from just a vision to today shipping millions of prepared meals to needy families and children in developing countries. You will be inspired by her calling, her vision, her passion, and you will forever be changed as a result.

I am honored to be asked to write this foreword and support such a wonderful cause. As the president of NuCerity International, I am proud that we have partnered with Gayla and Moms Against Hunger. NuCerity International empowers women (and select men) to become strong leaders who support not only their own significant businesses, but also enables them to become compassionate world-changers in concert with Moms Against Hunger.

My goal in writing this foreword is not just to encourage you to read this book. My goal is to challenge you and to ask you to step up, to give of your time, your money, your skills, talents, and education. I challenge you to develop an attitude of gratitude, and if you share my vision and the vision of Dr. Holley, select Moms Against Hunger as your nonprofit of choice.

Moms Against Hunger will continue to feed those in need and to support clinics, schools, and homes for the elderly. With your donation and your ongoing support, together we can make a difference in the world. Your association with Dr. Holley and your commitment to apply this book to your life will allow you to become the leader you were born to be. You will forever be a changed person when you engage with this organization, and tens of thousands of families less fortunate than you can benefit and go to sleep at night with food in their bellies because you care!

So let Dr. Gayla help you grow the leader within you. Let her be your mentor, your guide, your leader to becoming a global humanitarian. Read this book, and elevate your family, your faith, your business, and all that is important to you. Share the book with your friends and family members. Lock arms with Dr. Gayla and I believe you will experience a sense of love like you have never known. Allow Dr. Gayla to help you help others by determining what is truly important in your life and allow your faith to become your driving force to do good and give to those in need. I know most people have a desire to give in a way that changes lives and affects the lowest and most needful souls. Dr. Gayla will connect you, heart-to-heart, with those who need your help the most.

So get ready for an amazing ride. Get ready for real-life stories that will empower you, change you, and mold you into the complete leader I know you can be. Are you ready to begin? Good! Let's make this journey together, serving others for the greater good of all mankind.

Kevin Allen

Kevin Allen
President, NuCerity International

Dedication

I dedicate this book to all of the suffering people around the world in developing countries who don't know how to read and will never see this book. It is because of you that this book has been written. Your misery spurred my life into action to focus on making your lives better in some small way. I hope to educate many leaders in many nations to join hearts with me to find you and ease your pain.

It takes a mother's heart to love the unlovable, and a leader's heart to change the conditions in which you are living.

Acknowledgments

I would like to thank all of the many people around the world who have made an impact on my life. There have been so many who have walked through my life and each one has left his or her fingerprints of example and experience in my heart.

My parents, who had the courage to leave the safe shores of America and follow their hearts and calling. My husband who married a girl with dreams, your support has been unfathomable to help me accomplish them. My three brothers, who are my friends, your laughter and friendship is lifelong, and I thank you for supporting me to write some of our family history. My lovely daughter, thank you for sharing my vision and all the years of joy you have brought me.

To my many peers, friends, and supporters who walk beside me and believe in the hope that one day we can multiply Moms Against Hunger into the hearts of millions of moms. To Dr. Lonnie Rex, who gave me the courage to believe in what I felt in my heart. To the Founders of NuCerity, thank you for your support; together, we will create answers for children worldwide. To Kevin Allen, who reached out to me on that fateful day. And Phil Sheldon, who did his part to help kids by connecting us.

To Patrick Snow, who showed me the way to put fifty-six years on paper—your leadership has been effective and masterful to complete this book. To Tyler Tichelaar, your help on this book has been gratefully needed. To Shiloh Schroeder of Fusion Creative Works, thank you for the creative and special detailed work on this book. Thank you to Francesco Benvenuto for the stunning cover and the beautiful graphics you created.

To each of you, I am indebted, and you have a part in the pages and ages to come.

Without each one of you, there would be no record made or any story to be told. And to God who preplanned my destiny, I hope to make You smile within the pages of this book.

Contents

Introduction

Standing in front of a picture in my hallway at home, I was crying. It had been a tough season of hard work, ice cold weather, too many needs, not enough money, sickness, and abandonment by people. I don't know why I stopped there that day, but I stood there weeping, trying to look at the beautiful picture of a forest of trees with the sun shining through.

Gently, a quiet voice said to me, "Which tree are you?" And I really began to look through my tears at the trees in the picture. I noticed for the first time that the sunbeam was a shaft of light that shone down through the trees and landed on the very last tree at the picture's very edge. It was shining up the bark of the single tree that I had missed the whole time the picture had been hanging here.

He said to me, "You are the tree that I am shining on...."

I stopped crying and stood there amazed at His gracious words to me.

This incredible little personal experience was the turning point for me. Those words strengthened me at a very dark time of my life.

Many years later, I still have that picture—it means the world to me. And I shall never forget the words I heard that day. The picture on the cover of this book, *Growing the Leader Within You*, describes that picture.

You stand as if you are in a forest…with many people and issues like trees all around you. Through the many experiences of your life, there have been dark times for you as well. But a Light is shining down from above the tree line, and it's turning your history into the wisdom of leadership for tomorrow. *Growing the Leader Within You* uncovers those principles within. Look at the cover of this book and be encouraged! The Light is shining on you!

And just as I told a little baby boy I held in my arms in Fiji after he had just suffered the loss of his eye, "You WILL be strong, you WILL get to go home soon, you WILL grow up, you WILL be just fine." So I say those same words to leaders wherever you are in the world reading this book: "You WILL be strong, you WILL grow up, you WILL be just fine."

Growing the Leader Within You will brighten your pathway and shine Light on you. Each chapter is designed to teach a leadership principle to help you grow in the forest of life. From "Redrawing Your Mind Map" to "Identifying Your Coaches," this book will inspire you to take what life has given you and transform it into a pathway of guidance toward your goals and dreams. Your Passion will fuel your energy!

"The 20 Guidelines for Work, Life, and Faith" will define how reality brings destiny into focus. It is not a book filled with correctional positive how to's but one filled with actual stories and the corresponding hints and nudges that were directional actions leading to destiny. It's a blueprint of actuality and parallel wisdom that sharpened a compassionate heart into understanding how to help the world around all of us.

I challenge you to read it and personally answer the questions in each chapter. You will be amazed at the thread you find that was already woven into your destiny. This book is sure to shift your view of all of your experiences away from just being good or bad experiences into meaningful direction for the future.

Are you ready to activate? Let's begin right now....

1

Learning to Ask the Right Question

*One ought never to turn one's back on a threatened danger
and try to run away from it. If you do that, you will double the danger.
But if you meet it promptly and without flinching, you will reduce
the danger by half.*
— Sir Winston Churchill

THE AGENTS OF CHANGE

The day my parents brought me home from the hospital would be one of the worst days of my family's life. Arriving home in the rain, my young parents found a handful of welcoming guests at their house. My mother laid me down in my little baby bed and covered me in the new pink blankets and kissed me again. The guests congratulated my mother for a safe delivery and a healthy baby girl, never suspecting that their lives were about to be hit with an agent of change.

CHANGING CIRCUMSTANCES

The sky turned a dark greenish color and heavy thunder could be heard in the sky. The bare spring tree branches, bending and twisting, accepting the waves of violent air currents, told their own story of the drama unfolding. The family dog hid under the house and refused to come inside.

Walking over to a window and looking out at the sky, my dad suddenly saw the beginning twisting movements of a tornado gathering speed and coming straight for the house. "It's a tornado!" No time to get everyone in the car…. Much less go where? Standing still, his mind racing, my dad tried to decide what to do to protect his family and my parents' friends who were there with their two children.

MAKING INSTANT DECISIONS

Making an instant decision, my dad picked me up in my blanket from my little crib and pulled my two-year-old brother away from his toys. Calling urgently, he grabbed my mother and quickly ordered their friends to gather with him and kneel down beside the closet wall in the center of the home to pray for safety. The two young families, vulnerable to the raging storm, with their arms tightly around all of their children and holding their breaths, dreaded what was about to happen. *When you can't get out of the way of trouble, just turn and face it bravely.*

Deep rumbling noise, like a thousand planes flying low to the ground, shook the little house. The storm roared in, drastically changing our lives. Eyes tightly shut and hearts pounding, my two young parents didn't know whether they would be alive when the storm was over, or if they would be able to hold onto us children in the ferocious wind hitting the house.

My two-year-old brother looked up at our parents and felt their fear. Whimpering as my daddy grabbed him very hard and pressed him to his stomach, the child could hardly breathe in the fierce hug and the storm pressure he felt in his ears. They both bent over me, the tiny daughter, trying to protect my nose and mouth from the wind that seemed to be rushing in from everywhere. My little pink blanket flapped open and was closed with the quick hands of both parents as the twisting winds hit the house.

STAYING STILL IN THE STORM

Suddenly, the tornado slammed into the house like a head-on collision with a deafening freight train. The twisting of the wind ripped through the wooden beams of the frame house, shearing off the roof and shattering all the glass windows!

The walls, the windows, the ceiling, the lights, and even the electrical wiring was ripped up and disappeared into angry black clouds. My baby bed, the table and chairs, couch and coffee table were all swept up and disappeared. The house shifted on its foundation, and debris was swirling with bent metal pots, broken pottery shards, and all the many bits and pieces of our lives.

All of the house was damaged except for one very important wall, where two little families were kneeling. Everything was destroyed in that instantaneous moment. Even our pet dog had been carried by the wind out from under the house to somewhere high in the sky, never to be found again.

Pounding rain poured in as two families became soaked and shocked at the same time. The knifelike rain covered them in moments, and as they opened their eyes to try to keep the children from getting wet, they realized they had managed to hang onto all four children, and they were all still alive.

Children were screaming hysterically while parents tried to comfort them, wiping their faces with their own soaking wet clothing. Baby tears were mixed with the rain as the pounding wind subsided and the rain slowly let up. With nothing but their living bodies, they all slowly staggered to their feet, trying to stay calm. Peering through sodden hair, and constantly wiping rain from their eyes, they couldn't believe what they were seeing.

The entire front of the house had disappeared, and what was on the ground was badly damaged. But the four parents and four children were untouched by anything that had exploded next to them. Flying glass from the windows, airborne boards, and large metal pieces from the roof had slashed through the air, all missing each person in the melee of the tornado winds.

The young parents stood in shocked amazement as they viewed the chaos around them. The massive loss of their home and their belongings paled in comparison to the fact that they and the tender lives of their four little children had survived. It was the first miracle that would chart the course for my lifelong destiny.

FACING REALITY

My family never forgot the trauma of finding ourselves homeless in the pouring rain! In those days, there were no town shelters to run to that would house and feed families who had lost everything. There were no agencies that focused on helping families to recover from trauma and loss due to massive storms. Most families did not have much to share to start with in southern Illinois.

People in the town offered to let us stay with them. And our guests went back to their faraway home, never to be seen again for seventeen years! It took years to recover from the complete loss of all things, and we lived with handouts of other people's clothing, furniture, and household effects. Finding clothing to fit me as a newborn and my toddler brother was a small task compared to the overall responsibility of finding beds to sleep in each night while depending on other people to share with us their meager supplies. It took much time and effort for my parents to find another home, with the help of sympathetic strangers who offered rent money to start on. Finding food for each meal was a struggle because we were living on the generosity of others.

This experience was my introduction to life and to my miracle parents, Samuel and Joyce Latta, and my brother, Samuel Alan. I, Gayla Joyce, had been born just eight days before that devastating tornado.

ASKING THE RIGHT QUESTION

The most important question to ask after a life-changing experience is *not* "Why?" While it's natural to want to know the reasons why bad things happen to good people, it's a question that can only be answered later down life's road as we begin to sharpen our inward view of ourselves. Understanding the "why" seems to be impossible until you see the entire picture.

The most powerful way to view the agents of change that come into our lives is to start asking the right question. Asking the right question brings a new level of open understanding and a greater comprehension to life's experiences.

Many people have not found their answers to the "suddenly's" in their lives because they have not asked the right question. Asking "Why me?" or "Why did this happen to me?" does not provide the reason for the unwanted event. It only adds endless frustrations as the circles of "Why?" turn into tighter and tighter spirals of misunderstanding.

A constant misunderstanding of the experience can actually take us away from purpose and the reason for the happening because "Why?"

leads to "Why me?" When you begin to ask, "Why me?" you start down a road of fear and regression, which leads to dead-end roads that, of course, lead nowhere. Like railroad cars linked together on a train, the unwanted agents of change can start linking together as one event after another happens to us.

But asking the right question brings openness to the experience which will lead to wisdom for the future and better preparation when facing life's many ups and downs.

The right question, the important question to ask, is not *"Why me?"* Instead, we leap into future success by asking, *"Now what?"* Asking, "Now what?" opens the way through the confusion, the fears, and the self-doubt that cause us to find new and better ways to discover our destiny and live a fulfilled life. When the tornado was over, my parents didn't ask, "Why me?" They simply asked, "Now what?"

> *The pessimist complains about the wind.*
> *The optimist expects it to change.*
> *The leader adjusts the sails.*
> *— John Maxwell*

Asking "Now what?" opens doors that "Why?" questions never will. It's how to turn troubles into challenges that bring their own answers with them. This proper question causes the padlocked doors of "why" suddenly to unlock life's secrets. I have watched the leadership style of my family develop from many and varied experiences and have found that through life's unexpected moments and unplanned sudden turns, it was when we asked the most important question of all that we were able to move forward.

NOW WHAT?

Asking "Now what?" means you are looking ahead for the treasure in all of this. You are going to find surprises and unexpected goodness that will lead you further down your road of destiny. This question will give you positive wisdom and education for your fulfillment ahead.

The tornado turned out to be a mysterious precursor to begin my life with…a life filled with "Now what?" moments.

Later down the same road of unexpected challenges, an agent of change hit again when it was least expected. My husband and I were traveling in our brand new van, having just picked it up one hour earlier. We were so proud! It was silver with a baby blue interior, beautiful leather seats for four, and a couch in the back. We planned to fill our little fridge with food on our way out of town. We were headed for Canada for an extended trip throughout the North.

Driving with excitement, we were looking over our investment with proud joy when my husband said to me, "Lay back the seat and see how it does." I obeyed, and as soon as I was lying flat, I said, "Ohhhh, this is the life!" Suddenly, out of nowhere, a car in front of us lost control and violently swerved in our direction. Within moments, our van crashed into the car, demolishing it. Simultaneously, the semi-truck behind us plowed into us, forcing a collision both in front and from behind. The van's back doors crushed inward, and the nose of the big truck was literally inside our van.

Neither of us had time to put seatbelts on or brace for the impact. The steering wheel kept my husband from going into the windshield and because I was lying down, I didn't go over, but rather under the dashboard. Within seconds, many cars had crashed and a large number of vehicles were damaged. We were in shock! We had just gotten this shiny new van…. What about our investment? What about our trip?

But at that moment, nothing mattered except that we were alive and unhurt. Not even a scratch was on the two of us! "Now what?" we asked. It's didn't occur to us to start any kind of blaming of others. It had just happened. After the shock wore off, our question to figure out was "Now what?" It was an agent of change in our lives. We understood the value of each other, and how fragile our lives could be. We climbed out of the wreck, focusing on the needs of others who had suffered physical hurt.

GREAT OPPORTUNITIES CAN COME OUT OF TROUBLE

A pattern seems to exist for the instant troubles that suddenly throw us into a different mindset after a disaster. We can only assume at the moment the reasons for its happening. Yet tremendous upheavals and instant change usually result in the great solutions that move us further down life's road.

Life's storms definitely bring change to every person they touch, whether they are financial or health issues, weather-related, or unexpected accidents. The truth is that life happens to us all. It's who we turn to when it does, and what we do with it that affects what happens to us next. I have never found a sharp turn in the road of life that did not lead to a better way ahead.

> *Nothing can happen to us unless God lets it.*
> *And if He lets it, it will turn out for our good!*
> — Sam Latta, my dad

QUESTIONS TO PONDER:

1. Have you experienced an agent of change that came into your life and suddenly turned everything upside down?

_____

_____

_____

_____

2. Did you have to make some instant decisions that you may have always questioned in terms of whether you made the right choice?

_____

_____

_____

_____

2

Destiny's Puzzle

Great leaders are almost always great simplifiers,
who can cut through argument, debate,
and doubt to offer a solution everybody can understand.
— General Colin Powell

LOOKING FOR DESTINY

Your ability to ask, "Now what?" will lead to a better future made up of the woven colors of life in all of its switches and changes. One cannot imagine the adventures and lessons to come. Holding on to regrets leads to bitterness, but holding on to anticipation leads to a better tomorrow.

Little did my parents know what a big life they would live as a result of the tornado and all of the hundreds of thousands of people whose lives they would touch through their lifetimes! First, they had to move into a home with another family while they picked up the fragments of their lives to carry on. My mom tells of how they went back to the destroyed home to find any bits and pieces of their belongings. A dresser was crushed, but all the clothing inside it was still there. A book was found thrown outside, a small picture frame was broken but the picture inside was okay. Her Easter dress was found with the battered hat. *But material goods never had the same meaning again; they were just tools to be used in the moments of living life.*

My parents never could have known how their retelling of this traumatic event to me over and over through the years would slowly imprint in my heart the importance of helping families who suffer loss. Great leaders are not born; they are birthed through the fires of trouble, defeat, and loss. General Colin Powell tells of how leaders can see through many debates and doubts because of their own previous life experiences. **I can testify to the truth of that statement.**

Your own life may have dramatic events that turn everything you know inside out. And the quandary that follows can make you feel like you are sitting at a desk that has been cleared off and is now completely bare. What to do now? In my family's life, this situation was the precursor to a destiny about to unfold.

HEARING DIRECTION

One night, a single, mature lady came to speak at our church about her life as a missionary in Africa. She brought her slides, and as she was showing them and telling the adventures of what she was doing there, my dad watched the jungle pictures appearing on the screen and asked in his heart, "Where are the men? Why aren't any men going to Africa to be leaders? Why must a single woman try to do this huge massive work alone?"

A quiet small voice spoke to his heart and said, "You are a man; will you go?" He sat there, stunned at the quiet words that hit his heart like an atomic bomb, but he couldn't deny the truth that had been whispered to him.

My father told my mother of his call, and after much prayer and soul searching, my parents decided to answer it! Of course, their families were not very supportive, asking with concern, "How can you take four little kids to Africa to live in the jungles there? Aren't you afraid of what could happen?" Their outrage only made the decision to go that much stronger. My parents stood firm in their faith and decided to go.

When the urgency in your heart is stronger than the voices of those you love, press on no matter what is said. My parents picked up their destiny as if it were a puzzle, and they began to put together the pieces of how they might take their four young children and go to Africa. The plans started happening and the details of a major life change began—that would finally take place close to a year later. My family planned to be in Liberia, West Africa from five to seven years. By the time we left, Alan was nine, I was seven, Marvin was six, and Regan was five years old. Our parents were twenty-nine and thirty years old.

My parents' decision would have far-reaching effects we could not yet conceive. It would send shock waves across Africa that would affect hundreds of people, and it would forever imprint in my heart the need to help people. In fact, Mom and Dad would have their hands full with my brothers and me because all four of us were born leaders!

GATHERING PUZZLE PIECES

So many details needed to be taken care of before we left. My dad had to learn how to fly a plane, which he did between his speaking engagements to raise the funds for us to go. By the time we left the United States, he proudly had his forty hours of training done—from different airplanes and from all over America with different instructors. Supplies had to be brought, and we had to decide what to take that might be important, and what to leave. Having no idea what to expect, my parents could only imagine what they would need. Neither of them had ever been outside the U.S., much less to the jungles of West Africa.

There were health issues to consider. In the 1960s, disease and sickness were rampant so they had little knowledge of how to prepare children for the possibilities that might happen. Fortunately, the State Department provided the necessary forms and various instructions concerning contagious diseases, viruses, and what to do in life-threatening situations.

We would face danger of many sorts, including leprosy, tuberculosis, all sorts of airborne sickness, the dreaded malaria, and serious intestinal dysentery! I remember getting different shots through the United States Health Department. The shots had to be spaced out so our little bodies could handle the different vaccines trying to protect us from anything we might contract. Oh, how we hated those shots!

Strangely, we all suffered from every childhood disease that can be had during that preparation year. In fact, all six of us suffered the mumps at the very same time! I am sure my mother had a miserable year! But later upon arrival in Liberia, it was proven to be a great blessing that we had all been sick most of the previous year since children commonly died from childhood sicknesses such as the mumps or chickenpox in the jungle! Physically, we had been well-prepared.

PACKING SUPPLIES

So the painstaking job began of gathering up school supplies for the children. How much paper will we need? Pencils and crayons? How much glue will the children need? What kind of schooling will our children have? How does one plan for every detail to take enough supplies to live in a jungle?

There were equipment needs such as generators and tools, and lawn mowers and bushwhackers, chainsaws and cutters of every type. And the supplies that go with tools such as screws and nails, blades and sharpeners, and various belts and oils to accommodate whatever project Dad might anticipate doing.

Then there were ministry tools, such as Bibles (although no one could read where we would live—this did not enter the minds of those helping us to pack), my dad's guitars and my mother's accordion.

Finally, there were the personal things such as enough clothing for four growing children. (We planned to be there five years.) The boys could wear hand-me-downs from Alan, but Gayla could not wear her brother's clothing so special needs had to be considered. And what about food? How do we plan for that? So supplies of dried and tinned foods were prepared. And the different types of medications that might be needed. Household dishes, pots, and pans were the last to be packed as mother had to use them till close to the end. Toys were very limited and we children sacrificed to take only our fondest with us. Blankets, towels, and sheets were limited since it would be more important to have soaps and shampoos and toothpaste for us all.

FOCUSING ON ADVENTURE

To us children, going to Africa was a huge wonderful adventure! I can remember all the plans and work that went into making the arrangements for this journey to happen. We never heard the negative words of doubt, the fearful voices urging our parents to change their minds. We only knew the excitement and joy that Mom and Dad had about going to a strange land to help people.

General Colin Powell, who faced many obstacles in his career of serving, said, "Great leaders are almost always great simplifiers, who can cut through argument, debate, and doubt to offer a solution everybody can understand." He found that through any disagreements and arguments, leadership would always provide simple ways and answers for quandaries, which provided direction in spite of the confusion.

My dad told us kids that *responsibility was a privilege* and that we were the fortunate children because we were getting to go to Africa. That we would live in summer all the time and no more cold winters for us! Little did he know about the "summer" climate we would soon be "bathing" in. We believed his words and his mission became ours.

IGNORING THE OPINIONS

So while people watched and commented, my dad gathered five barrels and made wooden crates for all of our supplies. He painted them bright yellow with our names across each, just in case any of them should go missing upon arrival in Africa. Once my dad had a plan, he went after it with all his heart!

My philosophy of life is that if we make up our mind what we are going to make of our lives, then work hard toward that goal,
we never lose—somehow we win out.
— President Ronald Reagan

Finally, the trucks arrived to take our crates and barrels to the ship. And as the truck drove away with all of our personal belongings, it became apparent to all of our family and friends that we were going…no matter what.

We assumed that our crated supplies and five barrels of food would arrive a short while after we did. After all, they were leaving way ahead of us! And we prayed all of our precious cargo would arrive safely.

Little did we know that it would be many seasons before we would see our stuff again! I remember the many, many times my parents would say, "Well when the crates get here, we will have such and such." Oh, how we waited and longed for those crates to get there, and how we needed so many times what we had packed!

ACCEPTING SURPRISE

Our precious supplies were finally found after countless trips to ask at the port customs offices. But the crates and barrels had sat neglected for so long in an outdoor customs room that the humidity and rainy seasons had destroyed most of what was inside, leaving almost everything covered with mold and ruined. We thought we would be so happy to have everything finally with us. The clothes were still wearable, but they no longer would fit us. Every child was too tall with arms and legs having grown double in length from what Mother had thought would happen. And the shoes...? All completely ruined and moldy.

My brothers just passed down their shoes to each other, and then on to the African children, and Alan managed to wear a pair of Dad's shoes, but I had to go without proper shoes for a while. *Accepting surprises means to be able to manage if nothing goes as planned.* All the time we spent dreaming of the arrival of the crates didn't help them arrive any faster. Nor did it help when they arrived and we opened them to find new levels of disappointment to handle. Fully accepting the "here and now" can lead us to creative solutions (which we had to figure out in the end anyway).

The puzzle of putting a family's life together on a little village mission in the deep jungles of Liberia, while packing in Moline, Illinois in the 1960s, was a riddle to say the least. There wasn't much of a way to find out what was going to be there for us to use, and what was not possible to have. So we had just gathered up the different puzzle pieces of travel, supplies, training, and healthcare and decided to figure it out as we went along.

Have you ever felt like this? The questions seem greater than the answers. Not easy. *But accepting surprise works out in the end—just give it time.*

Years later, my husband and I would live as a young married couple in Southern Africa, cut off from our U.S. funding at the time. We were about to have a baby and had no money! The surprise of being left without any funding with a wife and baby on the way forced my young husband to create business even while we were living in the midst of a war. *This puzzle of destiny led to our independent success and took away our dependence on others to provide for us.* This lack was really our blessing in the long run!

EXCHANGING QUESTIONS FOR ANSWERS

Once when I was about to walk down a formal aisle in a ceremony in a ancient church in Budapest, Hungary, I realized I didn't have my white gloves with me. Now, this was a very formal occasion and the ladies were required to wear gloves.

Graciously, a lady behind me in the procession handed me one of her gloves and whispered gently to me, "Here, put one of mine on, put your gloved hand over your bare one and I will do the same with mine. No one will notice." Together, we walked in the procession, with our hands folded, and no one knew but me how thankful I was for her kindness. Her generous offer to a stranger is one of the personal memories that I came away with from that important trip. *Mature leaders invent solutions that often cost them their own comfort.*

> *When the lesson is ready to be learned...the teacher will appear.*
> — Buddhist Proverb

Have you noticed this principle of destiny's puzzle at work in your life? Somehow when you get to something you can't fix by yourself, something occurs either to help you solve the issue, or you learn something new at that moment, which changes your mind about how it should be done. When a dilemma comes to the forefront of our life, then the page turns and we find that we really didn't need it fixed, or we learn that the process holds another puzzle piece of wisdom that you wouldn't have found if it hadn't happened just like it did.

The "teacher" appears at that moment and shows us a new angle, a different way to look at it, and we discover that our understanding has increased about the whole thing. Our road of life takes a turn at showing us a greater measure of what is to come and how we will accomplish it. It's a broader brush than we were using; it's a bigger bucket given to us to share from our experiences in the drama of life. We become enlarged as a lasting result of the problem that faced us.

The puzzle to find your destiny may include:

1. Hearing or feeling clear direction for the future.

2. Going against the opinions of others who hope to keep you in "safe" surroundings.

3. Gathering details and looking for clues along the way about the place or occupation for which you are fitted. What small hints have been appearing?

4. Preparing for your future by focusing on learning, training, and educating yourself for the journey ahead.

5. Searching the soul to see what makes you laugh, what makes you cry, and what keeps you up at night because of the injustice of it all. My African childhood rewarded me with this kind of soul-searching—the most important part of the puzzle.

My questions to you in finding the pieces of your puzzle are:

1. Have you ever had a moment when the unexpected arrived and gave you a new way to think about solving something?

_____

_____

_____

_____

2. When you tried to act on that nudge or the impulse you felt, did others support or disagree with your idea?

_____

_____

_____

_____

3. Have you had any other experiences or any other clues pointing to this idea since?

_____

_____

_____

_____

President Ronald Reagan's philosophy in life was true. We *do* have to make up our minds about what we are going to do with our lives, and once we have the goal, we have to work steadily toward it lifelong. It is the blueprint of destiny, and what we were created to accomplish.

4. In life's unexpected twists and turns, what has happened in your own life that brought you to a greater level of understanding about the road you are traveling? And did that enlarge your focus in the direction you are to go?

_____

_____

_____

_____

It's like driving down a long road—every curve opens up a new view ahead. We like to think that once we make a decision to do something, that's it...it will remain just that. But rather, that decision slowly unfolds a new perspective and a different focus, bringing us to an altered understanding and the wisdom that comes to us from each event. You are not the person you were as a teenager, but rather development, life, and circumstances have shaped you into your present character. Neither can life remain the same; instead, it brings us new ways to look at life at each intersection with a "happening." Every decade opens a greater understanding about who you are, and what you are to accomplish on this earth.

These nudges in understanding pack into us the knowledge of how to help someone in need. It can be easy to miss the signs if the focus becomes inward and the thinking pattern stunted into self-protecting mannerisms. But it's when we look outside of our own day-to-day experiences that we can see the markings of a pre-planned destiny that started way back on the day we were born!

The head-on collision I spoke of earlier on our trip to Canada caused my husband and me to cancel most of the big trip, but it opened up a way to travel with some of my husband's family members whom I previously had not known that well. That trip gave me plenty of time to learn more about my husband's family and their view of life, which later served me well in understanding the family into which I had married. We never would have done this traveling together if not for the accident. *Loss brings its own gifts.*

And what was the lesson learned from the lady in the ceremony who had shared her white glove with me? Later, I found out that she was of royal lineage and held the title of "dame" in her country. Her little kindness to me as a stranger was a simple thing, yet big coming from an important leader in that lovely country. The little role she played in my life was an object lesson in kindness, for which I'm still grateful. My lack of correct protocol for the occasion showed me how to help another person with something so simple by sharing something of my own.

You have seen lots of life pass by you already, and the drama of it all may have been overwhelming. But to find the puzzle of your destiny and start putting together the pieces requires that you pick up the pieces and really look at them. Don't just avoid the mistakes or the losses but truly look at them and the hints they contain to show you the faint outline of an awesome future forming. You have all the clues already to help you decide what could be the greatest use for your life.

3

Letting Go of the Familiar

The hour is desperately dark, your flame is needed.
— Unknown

TRUSTING THE DREAM

The picture the assembled puzzle brings will bring you to the door of destiny. If you choose to face the future and open the door, it requires that you let go of the familiar. My parents were so enthusiastic about our great life change that it excited each of us children as well. My memories are of packing and packing and repacking, and of my parents making all kinds of lists, and calling their friends, and talking nonstop about what was about to happen.

As children, we watched a line of people come to admonish Mommy and Daddy. "Now if something starts happening over there, you get these kids out of there in a hurry!" Everyone stumbled around these words, trying to say, "If you need anything, get ahold of me," knowing that would be impossible. There would be no way to contact anyone quickly; nor could anyone help us when we would be on the other side of the world. We were about to jump off the face of the known earth to them. The day our family members came to see us off was full of conversations, anxiousness, and nervous packing. Grandparents came to say goodbye, all but positive that they might never see us again, their fears felt and verbalized. They had heard the dark land of Africa referred to as the "white man's graveyard." Nevertheless, my parents tried not to bend to their opinions and, instead, to stay positive on this last day with everyone.

And when the time finally arrived, each of us children was hugged and kissed with tears. One more bathroom trip...clean up the chocolate milk already spilled on a little white shirt...and we were ready. We were allowed to take one toy with us for the trip. Mother had to figure out how to travel some twenty-plus hours with four children, keeping everyone happy, clean, and fed with almost no provisions she could take for the journey.

Dressed in our Sunday best, hair slicked back, and polished shoes on, we lined up to get on board the flight that would, in some ways, take us backwards some three hundred years.

I don't remember what each of my brothers took on the Pan American plane, but I took my little blue Barbie case with three Barbie dolls inside. I held onto that small case the entire trip. Eating on the plane was exciting for us, and Mother made us stay presentable for the long trip. We had been told that after the plane landed, we would take a long ride in a car, then another plane trip before we finally got there. We had no concept of what this journey really entailed, but we were all going to become African missionaries, so the difficulties of travel did not enter our young minds.

Oblivious to Daddy's concerns and prayers, we simply enjoyed the long trip, eating with delight the little meals with tiny dishes and silverware on our trays and cups of water. We watched our parents talk while we tried to sip our little cups of juice and not spill on our clothes, tried to get comfortable while sitting straight up in an airline seat, and were told in hushed tones, "Just try to go to sleep," which was impossible to do. "Don't mess your clothes up" was whispered to us over and over.

I watched the smartly dressed flight attendants smoothly take care of everyone while wearing high heels and not having a hair get out of place. I wondered whether the African ladies would be wearing high heels like these ladies were. We enjoyed the exploration of walking down the aisle to the bathroom and trying out the little soaps and lotions. We washed our hands in the tiny sinks and looked with great anticipation in the mirror at our reflection as grinning children on the grandest adventure of our lives!

We giggled at every bump that happened; every roll of the plane felt like excitement to four children, but mother was not impressed and grasped her armrests with both hands each time any turbulence happened. Closing her eyes, she would hold her breath till the air currents calmed down again. *Her knowledge made her fear; our lack of knowledge made us laugh.*

Now, as an adult, I wonder what were my dad's thoughts on the plane. I am sure he was nervous, excited, and probably a little scared. After all, this whole adventure had resulted from his desire to follow the quiet voice he had heard. He had had the courage to trust the voice, the dream he believed in, and now there was no going back; he had taken his young pretty wife and his four little children out of America and into the unknown world.

I can imagine his thoughts: "Now when we arrive, I hope everything is in place and the other missionary is there to get us. What will I do if he didn't get the message? I hope I made the right decision taking

47

my family to Africa." Those thoughts must have circled around and around in his mind as the hours passed to the jet engines' droning. "Did I get everything we are going to need? Am I really doing this?"

QUESTIONS THAT HAVE NO ANSWERS

Dad took care of Mom and she took care of us. She was afraid of the plane ride; even today, she doesn't like flying, although she has flown millions of miles high above the earth, all over the world. Each time she has to force her fears down. Dad had his camera with him, so he took some pictures along the way. Later, he taught himself how to develop his own pictures, and we are grateful for his talents or we would have had no pictures of those precious years in our family.

We kids just kept asking, "Are we almost there?" Both parents had two children to watch over through the flight. Our questions were simple and based only on the present and what we were experiencing right then. As children, it didn't occur to us that time, connections, and people all have to match up or we would end up on a Liberian runway with no place to stay. But the questions my parents must have had at the time had no answers; my parents just had to walk out the experience, trusting that all the details were about to fall into place and everything would go according to plan.

Upon finally arriving at Roberts Field International Airport in Monrovia, Liberia, I can tell you as a little girl exactly how it felt. Some events become permanently imprinted on the mind when they happen, and that event was one of those for me. As the plane landed, we were all trying to peer out the oval metal plane windows to see anything at all. "We are here!" was everyone's first thoughts and words. As the engines died down and the noisy sounds ended, my brothers and I tried to jump up, only to have our parents tell us to sit back down and wait a little longer. Oh, it was so hard to wait as a kid!

OPENING THE DOOR TO THE FUTURE

Slowly, the door opened and the passengers filed out, each one silently looking at us as if we'd lost our minds to come to this place. My first memory as we stepped out of the plane and onto the ramp of stairs is of the incredible steaming heat. Having been raised in air conditioning our entire lives, we didn't know about real heat. When we stepped out the plane door and left the cool interior of that metal bird, it would be the last time we felt cool air for a very, very long time. We hadn't known how to appreciate air conditioning before.

The heat was so intense that it hit us like a wave, and then suddenly, it was a very sticky feeling, as each of us instantly broke out into a full sweat. The humidity was so high that it made the heat palatable. We had not been prepared for this opportunity to sweat! Mother and Dad each had two kids as we tried to go down the stairs with our toys and bags and not fall. I am sure those behind us sighed with impatience while waiting for our clan to get out of the way.

Once on the ground, I noticed the smell—like rotten burning rubber. The small airport was surrounded by a forest of trees; later, we discovered it was a rubber tree plantation. But the hot chemical smell masked the smell of sweating workers and steamy vegetation. We walked across the black tarmac looking at an old and dilapidated building. The terminal was filled with Africans all talking at once, greeting various people who had just come from the plane. As we entered, suddenly all eyes turned to look at the white family of six.

The smell of body odor was intense and made my nose water. The small closed-in building only intensified the smell, and the heat rising from sweating bodies made a lasting impression on this little girl. The bright African red, yellow, and green colors, garishly printed on the people's shirts and skirts, were a clear indication that we were in a foreign land.

Now what on earth would a white man and woman with four little children be doing here? Mom and Dad had no idea at twenty-nine and thirty years old what a far-reaching impact their decision to go to Africa with their four little children would have on every person they would come in contact with on both sides of the ocean. Curious, worldly eyes examined our clothing and shoes, assessing what we might have that they could use for themselves.

WHEN IDEALISM MEETS REALITY

Romantic and inspiring visions of helping a single African village had filled our parents' minds; they had envisioned helping to change darkness into light. Africa in those days was in need of outside help all over the continent. But the reality was that my parents had very little experience by which to gauge the peoples, customs, economies, and social rules of Liberia. My parents' idealistic view of helping these people did not include battling the generational curses of poverty and ignorance. They assumed the Liberians would welcome their help with open arms.

Watching the busy men going back and forth, unloading luggage, shouting orders for paperwork, and trundling various items around inside the building caused us to see a sort of a system at work. Confusion, melee, loud voices shouting to be heard, suitcases being carried here and there and back again, all made Mother a bit nervous as she tried to retain control of four rambunctious children who had been cooped up for too long and couldn't wait to start exploring. With her hand on all four of us, we nudged and jostled each other, looking and trying to see everything at once.

It would have been normal to us simply to walk through the airport and get into a cool car and continue the journey, but this was Africa and things mostly didn't go according to schedule. So we waited and waited, until our host, Missionary Bill Cupples, appeared to pick us up. In Africa, learning to wait is how it's done. Nothing happens in a hurry. The Cupples family had been here for seven years and would be going back to America after we got settled in. How happy Mr. Cupples was to see all of us! The long waiting for him was over...we had arrived.

Upon walking out of the airport, we were exposed to another set of lessons we would need to learn. I saw misery, hunger, filth, disease, beggars—poor, dirty, ragged people in desperate poverty, pain, and suffering, some with running sores, others without limbs, sitting on the bare dirt ground, all looking to us to give them something.

I saw dirty hands reaching out to us, pleading for help as we walked past. Our parents tightly gripped our hands and walked as quickly as possible to the car, the line of luggage being carried behind us. Dad kept turning to watch to be sure all of our pieces safely made it to the car.

From the first day, Mother started constantly saying, "Don't touch" and tried to keep her curious children from staring at the stark reality of suffering humanity. Our eyes were huge and our minds opened in an instant at the sights we passed on that short trip to the car. Old eyes of pain looked us children straight in the eyes; they begged for help, money, food, anything...just anything to help. Some stumbled to their feet to try to help us gather our things into the car, as if to say, "I can do something to help you."

Hurrying to bustle us into the car, our host told them, "It's okay; we've got them; you can go on.... No, don't pick that up.... Leave that there." The mass gathering around us wanted to help in some small way, to feel important. The hired porters waited for their money for helping us, but the ragged ones just expected a kind word.... Finally, getting the doors shut with everyone safely crammed inside the little gray Opel Kadett station wagon, and the luggage roped and tied on the roof, Mr. Cupples moved us from the press of people and turned our attention to views of trees and the road as quickly as he could.

But I couldn't focus on the surroundings; I kept seeing the old man with the heavily lined face and watery eyes with his twisted feet. His smile had shown broken teeth, and he had reached out a darkened, leather-like hand with blackened fingernails to me, but I had backed away. I hadn't even smiled at him; his pain had made me afraid.

I couldn't see the tall rubber plant trees passing us because I kept looking at the many bent-over women walking down the roads. They had babies wrapped in long cloths and tied to their backs. Big baskets on their heads were filled with sticks, and they balanced them while walking along the sides of the broken pavement, trying to avoid the traffic but staying out of the trees lining the road. Some of these women wore shabby tops and wrapped around skirts, some with raggedy holes or covered in dirt. Some were naked from the waist up. They never looked up…just kept their heads down, walking. I wondered why they were walking and not riding in a car like us….

The only paved road in the nation was the road to the airport. When we turned off of that road, everything changed. These roads were full of potholes, gravel, and often washed out or deeply rutted with truck tracks. We had to travel over thirty miles, which took over two hours because of the road conditions. It was just too hot to keep the windows up, so the dust billowed in, covering all of us in a gray sandy layer of dirt.

We started out from America looking like we were going to Sunday School, but now we were rumpled, sweaty, smelly, and wearing food and drink spills from our long flight. Mother just had to shake her head as she looked at all of us and wondered when and where we would get a bath.

Often we passed ragged and poor people who paused to watch the heavily loaded car struggle past. Their view of us was different from our view of them. *They saw provision; we saw need. They saw laughing excitement; we saw sadness and pain.* Idealism met Reality, and there seemed to be no way to meet in the middle.

There are people in the world so hungry, that God cannot appear to them except in the form of bread.
— Mahatma Gandhi

WHEN SIGHT IS BLINDED BY THE VIEW

Our family once visited the ocean beach in Liberia. I remember the waves looked so huge. The waters would fold over and build up into this high mountain before slowly spilling over and rushing down in a glory of foam and pouring water. The waves were so big that I would always want to stay close to the shore, afraid of the water's force. I wanted to enjoy the water, but the waves looked too high, and I didn't know how to swim.

My first view of Africa had a similar effect on me…tall mountains of need I was too little to understand; it only made me afraid. The sight of it all blinded my view. Suddenly, the laughing was over; I had seen the rough reality of Africa.

I wondered where the beggar I had seen at the airport lived. I could not conceive of the fact that he lived right there. "Why didn't he go home and get a bath to clean up?" I thought. I couldn't wait to take one. "Why didn't that lady just sitting beside the road go clean off that dirt all over her and her baby?"

We kept asking, "Are we almost there?" and finally, we arrived for our overnight stay at a place called Bomi Hills Missions. Several Americans lived there—Missionary Jack Langham, his wife, and two boys, Jacki and Larry; and two single women, Valda Russel and Ena Hilton—all dedicated to serve and teach the Africans. They were building a church and a school, and they had created a beautiful and inviting mission next to a dirty and noisy mining camp. The mission provided a true contrast between those who came to bless Africa and those who came to take from Africa.

The next day, we arrived at a gravel airstrip where we climbed aboard a small plane to head out for our new home. We had thought the little Opel Kadett was a tight fit for us all, but this little plane couldn't carry us and the luggage too! Someone would have to fly back for the luggage tomorrow. The control yoke was even taken out from the right side of the instrument panel to give us a little more room. Three kids and Mom squeezed in the back, and Alan sat on Dad's lap in the cockpit alongside Bill Cupples.

Tomorrow, my newly trained but inexperienced Dad would be flying this small plane on his own. Flying over the jungle, I could only see trees for as far as I could look. No towns, no roads, just deep green trees from the sky view. The sun was low in the sky and the lighting was still good so we were on time to arrive before dark, or so I heard the adults say. After an hour of flying over the mountains, we could see brown rivers curling through the jungle, but occasionally, a thin trail of smoke mysteriously floated upwards from some village beneath the canopy of trees. It was loud in the little plane, and Dad had to shout to say anything....

And when we saw the little dirt landing strip, I watched my mother look out the window at where we would be living. Her face never changed as she saw a poor village with mud huts and grass roofs beneath us. Looking down from above, she saw that we would be living some sixty-five miles away from any road, buried deep in the jungle with the Africans. We had come a world away from what she knew as normal and into a primitive environment with which she had nothing in common.

I never saw her expression change; nor did she say a word; she was sold out to this cause, 100 percent. Her courage gave me courage. Her peace gave me peace. And her ability to look for the good in everything would teach me to face life head on. She understood beauty, love, cleanliness, order, and God. What she was about to land in was ugliness, squalor, sickness, mud, and pagan beliefs. Those two worlds could not have been further apart.

And then we landed in Fassama. Bumping to a stop, we taxied up the dirt landing strip while our host pointed out various mission buildings we needed to know about. Soon we heard the sound of people running, clapping, and singing. Coming to a stop and opening the door, we could see a small group of smiling natives who were singing a song to us in a different language. With their voices all blending in harmony, and with big smiles on their faces and welcoming eyes to greet their new guests, they did their best to make us feel at home.

Next, they sang a song in broken English for us…. The leader said, "What wrong wit the Lattas" and the people said, "Not-ting." He said "Who says so?" and the people said, "We all say so!" It was their way of saying, "We like you." They were happy to see us…and reaching out with long arms, they helped each of us out of the plane. The majority of them were women who called out to us in musical voices.

Walking toward the mission, everyone was touching our arms, shoulders, and hands as if to say, "I'm helping you come this way."

Elsa Lund, a nurse from Canada, lived here along with Bill's wife and kids, Eddie and Ruth Ann. They all greeted us. Little Eddie had brought his BB gun along to the airstrip. He immediately handed it to Marvin, my six-year-old brother, who was fascinated with it.

When a big rooster came strutting across the airfield, Marvin took instant aim and shot it! Everyone stopped singing and looked at this little boy with a gun. The rooster had been hit in the head and had flopped over dead! Marvin had shot someone's rooster! We had only just arrived and, already, there was an awkward moment! The singing was over.... Everyone was looking at the dead rooster and Marvin in silence. No one knew what to do next!

To break the icy silence, Bill suggested we have chicken for supper. We did much later that night. Slowly, our little leadership band walked in the darkening shadows to our new home in Fassama, a village in Belli Chiefton, Liberia, West Africa.

I forget who carried the dead rooster.... I don't think Mother let us; nor was Marvin allowed to have the gun anymore. Soon the Cupples would leave Fassama and we would be left alone with Elsa Lund. She was an awesome lady who worked tirelessly to make the Africans' lives easier to bear. Without speaking their dialects, she communicated love and compassion, and they loved her for her work among them.

THE VIEW FROM THE PAST

Looking back, one of the things I wish we'd done was record every single detail of that first year in the jungle. But we were too busy living to think about the future and how precious what learning in the jungle would be for us in the future. When our sight is blinded by viewing what we don't understand, we are tempted just to look back to the past and think about how good it was instead of living in the moment at hand. It's a way the mind has of trying to escape current troubles.

In the beginning of our jungle life, when everything was new and exciting, we would think, "If only the folks back home could see us now." Oh the people, oh the living conditions, oh the way they did things here, oh the everyday adventures that were happening to us. But somewhere our thoughts changed to "If only I could see the folks back home now." Hardships and struggle took the joy out of living, and life became about surviving.

In America, our days had been spent gathering supplies, telling stories over and over, finding people to support our efforts, packing up our lives, and waiting for the day to take off. In Fassama, all that activity was done…we were here living in the dream. And we were seeing life's questions from a whole different point of view; many of those questions we could not answer. The actual hard work of living the dream had begun, and every day's focus became the work of that dream.

AMERICA MEETS AFRICA

The idealistic belief systems we came with did not fit the reality of the human beings living and suffering here. We had thought we would simply tell them the Gospel, live among them in love, help them understand a purpose for living, and build churches for them. But our beliefs and goals did not match with what they expected from us.

The natives' lack of education and knowledge kept them living in ignorance and fear, totally controlled by the Devil Bush Society, which, simply said, was a group of witch doctors. Finding any middle ground between Christianity and witchcraft was, and always will be, impossible. When fear grounds your feet, it's hard to fly. And when people believe in that fear, they will not move forward.

The country of Liberia, itself, had been founded to be a home for freed American slaves who wanted to return to Africa. In 1847, it became the independent nation of Liberia. The capital is Monrovia, named after U.S. President James Monroe. Liberia's people are loving, but they can be fierce when opposed. While the Liberian government wanted help from outside, competitive warring factions between tribes had kept the people in bondage to fear, witchcraft, and suffering.

Liberia had twenty-seven different dialects, so for our safety, we could not play favorites by learning to speak any of their languages. This situation was a huge drawback and often caused misunderstanding, but the only safe way for us to live among all the different tribes was for us to teach them English so we could communicate with them. And they all were eager to learn English from us.

Language is the road map of a culture.
It tells you where its people come from and where they are going.
— Rita Mae Brown

Teaching the Liberians English was challenging since many words in our language did not have a comparable word with the same meaning in their own language. If we were going to bring about change here, the first thing we needed to do was find common ground. And change for those deeply saturated in fearful tribal traditions of human and animal sacrifice is not an easy transformation to bring about.

CHANGING YOUR LIFE REQUIRES CHANGING YOUR MIND

Those early days of tribal living became days of earning the people's trust. Just because you tell someone, "I have brought you the answers to help you with this life," does not mean that your message will be readily accepted and immediately taken to heart. Our lives changed now from trusting our dream to learning how to gain their trust. To change your life requires changing your mind—how could we reach the place where they would change their minds when we couldn't speak their dialects? When the hour is desperately dark, your flame is most needed.

QUESTIONS TO PONDER:

1. Are you able to let go of the familiar to reach for the unknown dream in your heart?

_____

_____

_____

_____

_____

2. Can you accept that some of your questions will not have answers, and you will need to walk through life to find the answers as you go? What are your unanswered questions in your destiny?

_____

_____

_____

_____

_____

3. Have you prepared for adjustments when the door actually opens? How?

_____

_____

_____

_____

4. Have you trained yourself for the switch to happen from the ideal to reality?

_____

_____

_____

_____

5. Changing your life requires changing your mind. How have you prepared for this to happen?

_____

_____

_____

_____

4

Living in Raw Reality

Do whatever comes your way, as well as you can.
— Eleanor Roosevelt

OUT OF THE COMFORT ZONE

A dream and actual reality will not look alike in the beginning. But to make a dream into reality, first, we must lock into the facts and accept where we are; we must move out of the familiar into open uncharted waters where we will be impacted as well as make an impact.

In Liberia, living conditions were very poor. Sadly, how people lived in Liberia when we arrived in the 1960s is *still* the way people live in many rural areas of Africa. What looked to us like just haphazard structures placed this way and that really were not. The village had a center where the chief lived and ruled. He had the biggest hut with an area cleared out around it. And his wives were in different huts close by. He was in charge except when the witch doctor came. The witch doctor ruled above the chief's law.

There were never any plants in the village. Nor any trees. Just dirt. And sometimes a stray village dog that always looked so skinny and starved. I never saw anyone pay any attention to these dogs. The village was made up of huts, and those people who had goats for livestock had them tethered to their huts. No one had any large animals such as cows since the flies would bite and kill them, or the wild animals would attack them. Once in awhile, a hut would have to be rebuilt so the village men would help to restructure it.

The huts were made of stakes driven down into the ground and tied together with vines. Once the round structure was built, a clay and mud mixture would be flung on the sticks. Slowly, the "mud" would pile up, and as it dried, the natives would use their hands to smooth out its texture and make sure it filled all the gaps.

There were no buckets or tools—just the bare ground and many hands working together to create a new hut. The lack of tools hindered the people, but they didn't know what had been created in the modern world, so innocently, they used their hands. (I have seen a pastor paint his church building with just his bare hands and white-wash.) *The lack of mental knowledge causes great physical work.*

And when the walls were dry, then longer stakes were taken from the jungle trees, and cross-tied above the wall to create a cone-shaped roof. Then it would be tied together with more vines. These were not just little vines, but heavy, thick ones that when wet and soft could be shaped. When they dried, they would tighten and make a sturdy binding. Then the thatching of palm tree branches would be applied, branch by branch. The vines would be woven around the base of the palm branches, tying each one to the next until a very thick and waterproof covering was created. Unfortunately, many insects and snakes would live in the thatch roofing, which often created hazards for the native family indoors.

During the rainy season, it would pour for several months, bringing floods that could ruin the little mud houses instantly. So the people worked to make the mud thick and heavy to ward off the rainy season's ability to wreck their round huts.

WATCHING THE FIRE

Inside each village hut, in the center of the room, was a fire that burned constantly. The smoke would curl up into the thatch roofing, turning it black and creating a pungent smell of smoky sweat! There were no windows in the huts, only a small door opening, to protect against animals. The burning fire served as a deterrent to the animals entering the doorway. The people would sleep around the fire. Somehow, the height of the huts' thatch roofing kept them from catching on fire. These houses would last several years until the torrential rains would finally wash away their strength and need to be rebuilt.

The fire inside the hut was everything to the people. It represented cooking, light, and protection from the wild. It gave them warmth in the cold rainy season and something to look at day-by-day in the mud dwelling. It was the first and last thing tended each day; never was there a day off from tending the fire. In the jungle after dark, the stars are so bright and a full moon will light up the land with its cloudy light, but the Africans' fires would provide bright light to see by until dawn if needed.

The smells cannot be easily described. I can just tell you that there are descriptive words that come to my mind as I remember back to being inside those huts. Just simple descriptive words—earthy, sweaty, moldy, ashes, burning wood, sometimes the smell of sickness, and rotting plants and foods and dirt. It was dark inside with just a flickering flame for lights. But politeness and manners were paramount even there within the dank chambers of abject poverty. I have been in several of these huts as a child and again as an adult. They all smell the same, and I believe these rough houses with their close quarters add to the vulnerability of catching contagious sicknesses from each other.

To build a life, one has to use what is available and not mourn what isn't. *When a leader wants to accomplish something, the lack won't stop invention.*

MAKING A HOUSE INTO A HOME

Our mission area had been cleared out larger than the whole village area was. The village didn't seem to mind almost being in the encroaching jungle that grew aggressively. The missionaries wanted a wide berth around the mission's edges to keep all wild animals at bay and to see clearly who might be coming onto the mission and how many were coming. Our protection often depended on the ability to judge a situation carefully with as much time as possible so we did not make a mistake or offend some important person in the village. So the long areas of lawn, which had to be crossed before anyone could reach us, enabled us to be assured whether visitors came in friendship or anger. We manicured the grass, trying to use every means possible to teach the villagers about gardening, caretaking, and how hard work can pay off by having beauty around.

Our mission house was square but also made from mud and thatch. Inside was the main room with the kitchen off of it, two bedroom areas, and a bathroom with a homemade concrete tub. We had a water tower to catch water off the back of the bathroom roof, and gravity and our power pump coming from the river helped us to have water as needed. We carefully boiled all water for every use. My brothers shared one room while I had to sleep in my parents' room; at the end of their bed was a little small cot for me. Else Lund had her own small house near ours.

We had a running kerosene refrigerator, which was yellow with age, and an old fashioned woodstove to cook on. This stove had been hand-carried over the mountains by a hired porter and was greatly prized. Great risk to life and limb had been done to get these two tools into Fassama. Pauline Gruse had carved out this mission alone in the 1950s, and her vision to have something to make her life easier had also made our lives easier. *A leader's decisions and choices affect all those coming behind.*

We did have a few lights, but only for a precious couple of hours at night; they were run by a loud generator outside when my dad was home. Our furniture consisted of a simple metal table and chairs, a couch and chair, and nails with string for hanging our clothes on the walls. Very rustic and practical, it very much had a "camping" feel. We spent most of our days outside…the heat was just unbearable inside.

At night when all of us were safely inside, around a kerosene lantern, I remember many talks and family time. No television, no radio, certainly nothing of the modern world, but we had each other and that was really all that mattered. Mother would read long books to us—the classics; this entertainment helped all of us to cope with our strange world. She was the rock we all held onto. There were times when we could feel eyes watching us from the jungle—some human, some animal.

WATCHING THE FLOOR

The time came when our house floors and walls had to be redone. I remember watching the natives redo the floor, mixing and turning the mud and clay over and over with their hands to make the mixture to repair with. The hot humid air was thick with the rank smell of clay and mud. There is no hot weather like that of West Africa. It's so humid that the jungle fairly drips with moisture—as do the people who constantly have to mop the sweat off their faces just to see to do their work. This humidity makes everything grow like wild on the west tropical coast. But everyone persevered until the floor was done. I don't remember my mother complaining about the process. We just stayed out of the way while the experts did their magic. When the floor dried, it was shiny and smooth and polished like dark-colored cement. It was the only cool thing inside the house, but we were not allowed to go barefoot even inside because the bugs were a constant threat to us all.

Many times in the quest to fulfill a dream, you have to go back to bedrock and renew that foundation. That "floor" is the floor you stand upon as circumstantial tides try to erode away your vision and purpose. Destiny holds many episodes in destiny just like this example of refinishing the primitive floor. Side roads often waylay us in pursuing a dream and our resolve melts into the dripping chasms of uncomfortable living.

WATCHING THE CEILING

My mother and father would keep a watchful eye on the thatch roofing above our heads, watching for creepy crawlies, mosquitoes, biting flies, snakes, and spiders to drop down on us. Nightfall would be especially filled with night crawlers. Sleeping under mosquito netting was a blessing because we would be assured of a restful, bug-free night—even though the netting was so hot to sleep under and we children did complain about it! But mother's cause for worry was real, so she would not budge about the hot sleeping "tents"! We slept under mosquito nets each night in the jungle, no matter the heat. And our parents diligently gave us daily malaria pills to ward off the many bugs. I remember the ugly taste of quinine and how mother would try to grind the pills up and add honey to help the protective medicine go down. And when morning came, we did not simply put our shoes on; we had to slap them together first, making sure no scorpions or any other unwanted guests had made their home within our shoes.

Research in 2012 has shown that 3,000 African children die per day from malaria! A simple mosquito net could save many children's lives. I have never seen mosquito nets in African huts. The Africans simply haven't accepted that the mosquitoes that fly right past the fires built to keep wild animals out are biting them and their children in the night. This has caused such sickness and thousands of deaths for hundreds of generations in the bush across the vast continent of Africa. Mosquito nets are hot to sleep under, but with knowledge, they can save every life from malaria contracted at night.

Looking up can save your life. Look up when your destiny seems disjointed. To keep focused, one must always rely on the cause that sent you forward in the first place. My husband says, *"If you see something coming, do something about it."* Be aware of falling debris and areas of responsibility that require your attention to stay intact.

AREAS OF RESPONSIBILITY

Here are the areas of our small but important world each day. Each area was very valuable for different reasons for all of us.

Education: My parents operated a school at the mission, and it was filled with children hungry to learn. Most parents didn't seem to be interested in learning, but they allowed their children to be taught how to read and write and learn as they could or wanted. *Education is the key to unlocking the future for generations of people.* Education was the long-term component necessary to create the leaders for Africa's tomorrow.

Transportation: Our airplane, hangar, and airstrip. All were carefully maintained because they were our only way to get out of the jungle when we needed to. Dad watched over that plane and its hangar with his life.

Tool Shed: The older school children were taught how to run equipment and do simple gardening with our valuable tools. Caring for critical equipment often erupted in edgy nerves as the need to guard it was unimportant to or not understood by all of the students. The natives did not understand the need to keep the grass cut short (to keep snakes away), to put all equipment away each time (it will walk off when you walk off), and to maintain our precious equipment (we had no way to get new equipment). These areas often caused friction as Dad did his best to keep us safe in the midst of a dark place.

TWO WORLDS COLLIDE

Coming from two entirely different worlds, we and the natives learned survival from each other. They learned how to make better structures to live in from us, and we learned how to survive this climate from them.

Mistakes are made by the best of mankind; after all, we are all human no matter where we live in the world. The church was in the village; it was the only square building with an actual metal roof, and that roof was not a good idea because when it rained, the sound was so loud that the speaker couldn't be heard well. And in the hot sun, the contracting tin would make all kinds of popping and cracking noises, causing everyone inside to think some animal might be on the roof about to drop through! It's funny to think about now, but the distraction only added difficulty to a situation where there were already communication problems. It would have been much better to build a thatched roof that softened the sounds and offered much better insulation from the burning sun. A wheel axle hung in front of the church, and when it was time for the service, someone would beat the steel hub and people would come to see what it was about. (No set time schedule existed because no one owned a watch.)

The Africans were distant but kind to us, and they were also curious about us. Many of them had never seen a white girl with blond hair, so I was touched often and my braided hair sometimes pulled. Without being able to speak each other's language, we used lots of smiles and gestures to communicate. I'm sure my parents experienced a lot of cautious moments while watching the native people examine their daughter and sons.

A former cannibal lived close by who had all of his teeth sharpened to points. His name was Si. Others had unusual names, such as one man who was called Sunday, while still others had simple nouns for names. Occasionally, a pygmy man would come through as his tribe hunted in the jungle. None of these people knew dates and times, so they didn't know when they were born or how old they were. Years and ages were totally unimportant to them, but the aged were treated as the significant ones.

With our own garden and chicken yard on the mission, we did the best we could to feed ourselves, but often, we found our supplies raided by bugs and animals. We raised our own food and lived without electricity during the day. And we dressed simply to try to combat the heat. We only owned a few garments each, and washing was an ordeal down by the river for the girls who helped us on the mission each day. Often, we kids looked ragged from running around, but we appeared very wealthy in the eyes of the natives who wore nothing.

My dad used a generator at night for several hours to try to contact the outside world through a ham radio system. Our lights would remind us of home, and that the modern world still existed for us each night.

Being children and living outside most of the time, we often would be exposed to different contagious infections by the adults and children around us. I remember mother spraying down the wall and door after a leper had come to our house looking for food. No scratch or cut was ignored because the tropics could turn a simple cut into instant disease. The jungle's germs were aggressive and deadly. Mother would look us over while bathing us every day. Nothing was ignored.

One time, Alan suffered serious second degree burns that left him with blisters the size of golf balls. I was bitten by an angry monkey, and Marvin was later hit by a car in the capital city, but nothing ever touched our baby brother Regan. Fortunately, none of us children suffered anything lasting, as a result of God's hand on us.

Early mornings in the jungle were always filled with the melodious sounds of thousands of birds calling out the dawn. Between the birds calling, the screeching monkeys, and the roosters tooting their own horns, morning was noisy but good. It was the coolest part of the day, and the rising sun always put a special glow and freshness on everything.

It's not what you have that makes you rich, it's what you don't have.
— Gayla Holley

LOOKING WITHIN TO FIND WHAT MATTERS

As a family, we learned the freedom that comes from not having much. *It's actually quite freeing not to have very many possessions.* The Western World is so busy tending to material goods and possessions that there is no time left to enjoy just being alive.

Having a palace for a home means constant upkeep, repairs, keeping insurance on it, surveillance and protection for it from thieves, cleaning it, updating it, organizing all the stuff inside of it, and having a trusted staff to manage it all. This wealth can absolutely consume us!

Andre Gide, the French writer, humorist, and moralist who received the Nobel prize, said *"Complete possession is proved only by giving. All you are unable to give possesses you."* Possessions are meant to be used, but much of the time, we in the twenty-first century are being used by our possessions.

My late father-in-law, Rev. E.L. Holley, used to say, *"If you have 100 cows…the cows really have you."* Because you must spend part of each day taking care of them, feeding them, providing for them, servicing them, hauling them around, finding them when they get lost, seeing to their veterinary needs, and a host of other details.

It seems the more I have in my life…the less I have of me. So the point is to look within and see what would really matter if everything else were gone. What are we willing to spend our time doing when we realize we will never be able to get those hours back? These are the heart questions of predetermined sacrifice that must be asked when pursuing a leader's life.

QUESTION TO PONDER:

1. If you had to turn a house into a home, but couldn't buy a thing, and had to use what was already inside of it, how would you accomplish this amazing feat?

_____

_____

_____

_____

2. Tending the fire means: What is the main focus in your life and how do you keep it alive? That which feeds us, protects us, and gives us light must be protected.

_____

_____

_____

3. When the outside world and the inside world don't match, it's as if two worlds are on a collision course. The inner world must dominate the outer realm. If the outer world is stronger than the inner one, collapse can occur. How do you feed and strengthen your inner world?

_____

_____

_____

4. Take a piece of paper and write down a list of things. If everything had to be removed so you could accomplish your dream, what could you give up? Forget the how to's of making it happen; just write down the facts of what could be.

_____

_____

_____

5. Looking for leadership to trust? Who is a bridge builder who has been willing to risk his or her own wellbeing to help you dream?

_____

_____

_____

5

Traveling Companions

Perhaps you do not understand me because you do not love me.
— African Proverb

CHAIN OF COMMAND

When the outside and inside world do not match, other leaders can come to help you see your vision through different sets of eyes. These different viewpoints are invaluable because they help you gain a perspective that deepens your understanding of leadership. These people serve as mentors and guides to us along the way.

No one will reach his or her destiny without the help of others. And often years later, those silent memories speak again the wisdom we gained from eyes and ears that have gone ahead of us, wisdom that now comes back to help us in our life work. They serve as traveling companions and mentors for seasons of need in our lives.

Taking you to the village and showing you around is my way of helping you to see the actual world of jungle life. A clear chain of command existed in three areas: the African chief, the witch doctor, and the missionary leader. The chief provided leadership by the heritage of his birth, the witch doctor led by using fear and darkness to control others, and the missionary provided leadership out of the pure love of the Gospel. These were the traveling companions of the simple African. What hatred and fear, disease and plague, poverty and nothingness, ignorance and loss could not conquer, Love did.

Liberians would not readily accept the word of the outsider over those of the generations of leaders they had believed; instead, they would test the man to see what he was made of, even though at times they had to admit the missionary's word was better than their ancestor's word. They would spend years with one foot in this new river and one foot in their ancestral river, never making the clear decision about who to follow. *Progress cannot happen when we don't make a clear choice.* And their traditions often blocked them from new understanding.

The elders in the villages would advise their people to stay in the old ways. Our advisors, who had dealt with African traditions, were invaluable in providing us information and wisdom for understanding the Africans' ways.

The place where the three types of leadership touched was the language of pain. The Africans suffered much physical pain, partly due to the rugged environment and partly due to the lack of education. The witch doctors had the majority of influence, keeping the villages under their control with their various shells and beads, human and animal flesh parts, ashes, and other bodily fluids to "cure" people of their different maladies. These men practiced evil in various ways while blaming people, their emotions, or the white man for death or disease. Yet they could not combat serious sickness with their potions and incantations. The chief would look at the white missionaries to see whether they could offer aid. When this happened, it was the break in the dam that the missionary needed to step in and offer help.

Else Lund went to Liberia as a young woman to serve the needs of Africans in the deep jungles. She spent thirty-seven years of her life in West Africa among the natives, touching them with compassion and tender loving care. Other young women like her gave up personal lives to become servant leaders as medical missionaries for people in need around the world. Interestingly, the village elders seemed to tolerate a woman coming into their world and offering medical aid, even though women were only servants and had no rights in the village life at large.

In 1875, Henry Fowle Durant, founder of Wellesley College, believed that God was "calling to womanhood to come up higher, to prepare herself for great conflicts, for vast reforms in social life, for noblest usefulness." During the nineteenth and twentieth centuries, women have sometimes numbered more than two-thirds of the missionary force around the world—women in leadership positions like Amy Carmichael, Adele Fielde, Johanna Veenstra, and Charlotte Moon, who led for decades in China, later to die of starvation. Mary Slessor, who later continued the work of David Livingston in Africa in 1875, has a legacy that lives on today in Nigeria. Elizabeth Elliot served in South America, and Helen Roseveare was a missionary doctor to the Congo. All were women leaders of the finest caliber who served well and answered their call to serve humanity's physical and spiritual needs, doing so very faithfully and alone. And, amazingly, all of this happened at a time in history when women were certainly not able to have the freedom of leadership we have today.

SOMEONE TO BELIEVE IN

Else had a little house next to ours in Fassama and lived there caring for the sick and teaching in the school each day. She was a tall and slim Canadian woman who put the needs of others before her own. Gentle and calm, she moved among the people with quiet but great authority. Her ability to make African women understand the need to clean, wash, and care properly for their children was unprecedented.

I greatly admired Else. I would watch her walk among the natives and touch them kindly, looking at them and their children with love. She didn't speak their languages, but she spoke to them in a language of love. Early on, I decided to be a nurse like her.

Else was in charge of the small humble clinic we had there in Fassama. It was just a little room where she would see patients whenever she was not teaching in the school. Sometimes, people could be seen sitting outside, waiting in pain till she could see them. She kept bandages, ointments, and a few precious medications there to treat impossible situations. Soap and water were her two greatest lessons to show and tell.

I looked up to this tall angel, wondering how she touched all these people without concern for herself. Her hands were tender and the natives could feel her heart toward them. Her eyes filled with tears as she would treat a wound with the greatest care and respect for the person. Helping women in childbirth and holding sick babies in her arms, Else touched so many lives with healing grace.

Else believed in miracles and often would pray for her patients when she had nothing to use to help them. How overwhelming it must have been at times for her to see such huge needs and have no modern medicine to ease their suffering. But her presence and caring touches while she washed nubs of fingers and stubs of leprosy-eaten feet made her greatly loved among the Africans.

USE ACTIONS NOT WORDS

The sights that Else saw! The people's needs were overwhelming, even to me watching as a child—I knew she needed helpers. She took care of open wounds and broken bones, high fevers and malaria cases. She tried to help people dying from dysentery and mysterious diseases of all types. I saw her care for lepers without fingers or toes, some in such terrible conditions that I remember their poor sad eyes. Her life was filled with helping the ragged helpless. That became what I wanted to do…help people in need. She saw the need and did something. And her doing was being seen by the people and gave her Christian message great authority among them.

Before the missionaries came, a pregnant African woman would wear the witch doctor's medicine around her neck, go work in the fields, go into labor, and birth a baby right in the field. Then sit up afterwards, alone in the field, strap the tiny baby on her back, and go back to work in terrible pain. More often than not, she would suffer the anguish of her newborn's death. The work of women leaders was crucial in helping these women to understand healthcare for themselves and their children.

Do not wait for leaders; do it alone, person to person.
— Mother Teresa

MY FIRST TRAVELING COMPANION

One day, I made myself a promise to get up extra early and go work with Else all day. I did not ask my parents if such a thing would be allowed. My assumption was that as a little nurse, I could do what was needed to help.

So one morning at daybreak, I got up and slipped out of the house, without waking up anyone. I walked quietly to the clinic, alone as a little white girl in the twilight morning shadows. While walking quietly, I was excited about my day and what Else might let me do to help. No natives tried to stop me; they just watched me walk past them—surely, they were wondering, "What is this child doing?" But no one touched me on that early morning walk.

When Else saw me at the clinic, she already had a line of patients waiting at the door. Since she was already busy taking care of someone, she quietly asked me, "Why are you here?" I told her, "Because you need some help." Being too busy to stop and take me home, she simply replied, "Do your parents know where you are?" My answer to that was a nod. So she gave me bandages and water and told me to help her wrap up the wounds on the next person.

I knelt down right beside Else on the dirt floor. I put my hands in the same metal basin of soapy water as she did. I tried to wash the wound as tenderly as she did. The man's leg looked like some bad accident had happened to it while hunting. He didn't care who was helping him; he just wanted the pain to stop. So our hands washed out the wound and bandaged him up. We could not speak his language, but he could tell from our hands and care that we wanted to help him. His painful eyes watched my little hands wash the wound and try to help. He never moved, nor smiled, but he allowed a girl child to help him in his need. He didn't understand our words, but he knew we loved him because we helped him. Else would tell me, "Just use your heart to treat them."

USE YOUR HEART

I was really enjoying myself, going from person to person with Else. I copied her in patting the patient's arm or leg. A happy feeling was in my heart because I felt like I was helping Else and the people in need. Even as a seven-year-old little girl, I could see that these people needed food and water. Looking at the distended belly of a child suffering with malnutrition made my own growling tummy unimportant.

Else was patient with me, along with her suffering patients. She kept me close by her side, and together, we washed arms and legs, wiping bloody bandages and soothing coughing fits. I could have stayed there forever doing that with her! I was enchanted and thrilled to be doing something important with her. We treated each person like he or she was the most important and sickest patient in a real hospital. I held babies with high fevers, and made coughing children drink things she handed me to give to them. She mentored me and never knew it. She cared for the sick with an extra pair of little hands beside her. Her hands taught mine how to love the unlovable. She was a companion who marked my young life forever.

Still today, Africa and many other parts of the developing world have epidemics of various diseases, with AIDs killing thousands daily. A huge amount of information about the health of those living in poverty around the world can be studied by those who feel compassion for this area of work.

CURABLE IGNORANCE

Much of the time, lack of knowledge was what caused so much disease and sickness among the people. The river near the mission and village was contaminated with deadly bacterial infections and viruses. All along the riverbank for hundreds of miles, small villages had been created to have water access. And the people in every village would use the river's water for everything. They would scoop water into a large pot for cooking. Daily, we would see naked people bathing in the muddy brown water. Mommies would wash clothes with lye soap in the water and pound the clothing with a rock on the banks, letting the suds fall back into the water. And all of them daily used the river for their bathroom privileges without regard to who was watching.

These activities were done without a thought. The only caution the people would take was to watch for deadly water snakes come swimming downstream, which would instantly cause people to scatter out of the water. The villagers up and down the rivers thought that because the water moved past them in a current, their water was "fresh." They never considered that people were upstream and downstream from them. The compounded bacterial strains and viruses that resulted are staggering to consider. This lack of knowledge is the cause for much waterborne illness across Africa, and it's completely curable with education.

LEARNING LESSONS OF OBEDIENCE

A rude awakening occurred for me when two very upset parents sounded the alarm throughout that Gayla was missing! When I was discovered at the clinic with Else, their relief and my personal discomfort was huge! Why were they so upset? Being a nurse had been my only thought, and it was my responsibility. Else lost a good right hand that day, although she kept a smile on her face through the loss of her only small employee.

Only later did I understand that my safety was at risk. Our village was in close proximity to the Devil Bush Society—the dreaded witch doctor's personal lair. Recently in the capital city of Monrovia, a white child had disappeared and been used for sacrifice purposes. Once I understood that, I never left my mother's side again, even though my heart was drawn to helping Else. *Sometimes we are removed from our desire for protective measures for the future, but the seed gets planted in a single experience.*

A MIRACLE FORTY YEARS LATER

Some forty years later, I suffered a lung illness and went to see Dr. Unger, a well-known and respected pulmonologist in Clear Lake, Texas. After running x-rays and an MRI, he brought me in for a consultation to see my results.

He asked me whether, as a child, I had ever been around anyone who had tuberculosis. When I told him where I had lived as a child, he nodded his head and told me that confirmed his report. He looked at me strangely and said, "I've never seen a case like you before…. I see a shadow that looks like the shape of a hand that's over this area we are looking at. It's as if something has stopped tuberculosis from colonizing in your lung." I told him with a smile that I knew whose hand that was and probably when it happened. That it would be Jesus' hand from when I had been a seven-year-old little girl, helping people in need. He looked back at me and said, "Go home, sing all you want, sing all you can; I never want to see you again!" I couldn't wait to hug him!

God never forgets what is done to help the suffering in the world, and He always repays in the most personal ways! Just because "facts" seem to be in charge of your life, when you know your destiny and work toward that goal, the truth will prevail no matter what happens! *Facts can change from day to day…but truth never does.*

While reading this book, something may come back to you that is a connecting link to what you wanted to do as a child when you grew up. Look into your history to see whether your leadership bend has not been in the same direction you are now working in as an adult!

MENTORSHIP

Your ability to lead others is only as good as your relationships with people. You may already have determined your destiny DNA, so you are focused on getting to your goals. That's great, but as a leader, one must remember this phrase: "I'd rather be a little part of something big, than a big part of something little." We can be the big dog on the porch, but if that's the point, we will not get the bigger picture of true leadership.

Leadership is not just getting our goals met; it's also about bringing as many people into our vision as possible so it can become their vision too, spreading influence around the world. We will not be able to multiply our ideas if we only believe in the power of ourselves. All the people in all the nations are our neighbors. Many compassionate leaders are now trying to push the word out about the serious needs on earth, and there are things you can do to help! We are our brother's keeper. Leadership is influence.

In your awareness of being a leader, you must look at who are your mentors as well as who you are mentoring. Both have been put into your life. The mentor is in front of you, pulling you ahead while the ones you mentor are following behind you, being drawn along by you. A mentor is an unforgettable person who is not necessarily a friend, but more like a coach.

WHEN YOUR WORDS RING IN OTHERS' EARS

Nona Freeman was such a lady in my life. She was a strong leader in every sense of the word. She and her husband went to Africa in 1948 with five children, ages nine years old to six months. She taught herself to speak Afrikaans in South Africa, and she traveled the length and breadth of the African continent to serve people. When her husband was killed in Kenya in a tragic accident, she did not let it crumble her. She kept on traveling and speaking around the world. She had to eat a special diet, but she never allowed it to dictate where she went or who she was as a person. She mentored thousands of young leaders through her teachings and writings.

While on trips with her, Nona taught my husband and me old African ways and how to step over our own culture to get to common ground with the locals. It was she who taught us how to smuggle food into nations so it would get through to those in need. She was bold and courageous and full of fun! Things that others found dangerous she looked at as adventurous. She had figured out ways to go around greedy customs agents to keep precious goods from getting into the wrong hands. She would freely share her knowledge with us, knowing we would need her wisdom in Africa. Her ability to teach us came from the rich experiences she had already been through herself.

In tough times, Nona would breeze through our lives, offering wisdom on everything from food to how to lead the leaders we were dealing with. Her constant joy even when things were tight and frustrating was her sense of humor that often would break the tension. I loved her.

As a young couple about to have a baby in the battlegrounds of Zimbabwe, Nona intended to be with us and kept close contact as we got closer to delivery. She offered advice and counseled me, helping me prepare for the life-changing event of having a baby. She made it seem so natural to be in a foreign land at war, having a baby without my mother beside me. Her way of supporting me gave me courage that I could do it and she would help me.

In the end, Nona couldn't get to me, so we went through our baby's birth alone. But remembering her many words kept me centered as if she were there in person after all. Now that's the power of being a leader.... When your words ring in the ears of those following you as if you are there speaking to them, you have mentored them well.

As a younger leader watching her, I found Nona to be my greatest positive influence in a leadership role. She would just laugh at difficulties, and offer advice after everyone stopped laughing. And then she would pray. Her knowledge of how to keep others inspired was a skill amazing to watch. When she was with you, it was as if no one else mattered.... She was with you. She was in demand wherever she went because she had mastered the art of being a leader. Everyone wanted to be alone with her because she had a way of making people feel like she cared for their families just like they did.

Once when we were on the road with Nona in South Africa, we were hungry, without any food or a place to find food to eat. She showed us how to feed ourselves in a pinch. By watching her drive, she taught us how to watch for small birds on the road. She managed to hit a guinea fowl with the car; then she stopped, picked it up, wrapped it in foil (which she had in the car), lifted the hood of the car, laid it on top of the engine, and closed the hood. Laughing, she got back in the car and drove on! After several hours, we stopped and opened the hood, taking out the now blackened package. We opened it and had a grand dinner alone right there—just the three of us.

At times, it wasn't so much what she said that impacted us; it was how she did the unconventional, showing wisdom in the circumstances we were all in that shaped us. *Actions are the greatest lessons we learn from others, not words.*

Later in life when we felt we needed to make a major change, Nona and E.L. "Bug" Freeman were our greatest allies and the only ones to support our decision. They came to spend time with us and gave us their blessing. Their ability to look past popular opinion to see the heart of a matter was an invaluable treasure of mentorship to us both.

We loved the Freemans and will always hold them in high regard—they *always* supported us and encouraged us to follow God's direction for our lives. For that, I will always be indebted to them!

Others along the way have also offered us kindness and a helping hand. Finding them, however, was rare because leaders who looked out for other young leaders were not common in the places where we traveled. Most people are focused on themselves rather than the young who watch them from the sidelines.

There will be good and bad mentors all along the road we travel, but both are teachers in life. Finding what I thought would be a great fit for a friend in a older woman, I gave her access to my heart. I believed in her. She was older and more knowledgeable than I, so I made time to spend with her. She seemed interested in my friendship as well and together we had long talks and often shared hearts. Then one day, she apparently decided that she no longer wanted to be friends, and I was cut off. I was devastated and felt betrayed. I was truly a friend to her, but she had had another agenda. I learned a painful lesson through that experience. Just because someone is older than me, does not make her wiser. While older people have certainly lived longer, they may have become well-trained in how to manipulate others. I came to the conclusion that I had been used, and I had to let it go for my own good and peace of mind. *Older does not mean more mature.*

MENTORING MEANS ME

If it's going to be, it's up to me.

After several tries with other older women, my heart concluded that I would not find any mentoring help from them. Over time, books became my traveling companions. I learned from experiences on written pages what good leadership was. And then I used that knowledge to mentor the young who were watching me.

One's children should be the ones to mentor over any others. So when motherhood came and my daughter was old enough to attend school, I made the decision to home-school her and pour into her everything I had learned along with her regular studies. I became her traveling companion as well as her mother. And finally the day came when she graduated. I was so proud—it felt as if we both graduated!

The first and most important people you will ever mentor will be your children. They are learning from you both the good and the bad. It is a caution worth sharing that as leaders, we should not look over the heads of our own flesh and blood to mentor others.

Your seed has the possibility of carrying on your work after you have passed away. And your children's children can certainly be touched by your directives and mentoring abilities. President Abraham Lincoln famously said, "The written page is the only way the dead can teach the unborn." Your leadership can be passed down for many generations when you become a mentor.

Now that my daughter is in her thirties, she often amazes me with her skill, her ability to lead well, and her multi-tasking talents. And when I compliment her, she always turns to me with that beautiful smile of hers that still takes my breath away and says, "Mom, you taught me this when I was little…." I am so very thankful for the many years of home-schooling and the thousands of seeds that were planted in her heart to teach her that we are to be responsible citizens of this world and make a difference every day in the lives around us.

If relatives help each other, what evil can hurt them?
— African proverb

Once during a disaster, I was setting up feeding tables when I saw a woman who was aimlessly wandering around in a daze, having been driven from her home, which was one of the thousands burning down. So I touched her on the arm and asked her whether she'd like to help me. She agreed and I put her to work right away. I knew it would take her mind off what she could do nothing to control and offer her a comforting distraction from this terrible hour in her life. She had no family to come be with her; sadly, I see this broken link in a family chain often.

That form of help became a pattern I followed for many years to come. Give someone in need a task to do so the person is strengthened and you are helped. Mentorship can take on many faces; the point is to reach out to someone you can help and simply start helping him.

The old woman looks after the child to grow its teeth, and the young one in turn looks after the old woman when she loses her teeth.
— African Proverb

Learning the proper chain of command in the society you are involved with will help you as a leader. And your ability to follow a traveling companion certainly teaches you how to mentor others behind you.

QUESTIONS TO PONDER:

1. When you were a child, was there someone you looked up to with whom you felt a strong bond? What did that person do that inspired you?

_____

_____

_____

_____

2. Who has been your traveling companion and mentored you?

_____

_____

_____

_____

3. What has been the greatest lesson you learned from this person?

_____

_____

_____

_____

4. Those you have had to pass by have also taught you something. What was the greatest lesson you learned from them?

_____

_____

_____

_____

5. Using language is only part of communicating leadership; "heart" is the other part. Do you find it easy to use this language in leadership?

_____

_____

_____

6. What is the chain of command you have seen in leadership around you? Have you been able to impact that leadership for good?

_____

_____

_____

6

Redrawing Your Mind Map

African travel requires three things: a strong will to live, navigational skills, and a creative imagination.
—Gayla Holley

TRAVELING OPTIONS

Navigating travel systems is important to a leader. Your strength to move ahead—using what is available leverage for your life, work, or faith—depends on your skills. No matter where you live, your life can be like living in a jungle filled with strange happenings, challenges to somehow break through, people who can sometimes be likened to animals, and a hostile environment to survive in. Understanding your traveling options to get through the jungle will require knowledge, and at times, your life will depend on learning lessons of obedience. You will need a mind map to sort out the tangles and turns along the way.

Traveling through the maze of opportunities, many of which are often distractions to our purpose, demands that *the basic will to survive* be stronger than the opposition in front of us. Our trained ability to traverse through difficulties means there has to be a mind map to follow. If you are the one charting the course, your carefully noted experiences can become a mind map for others to follow down the road. Otherwise, the training you receive will *need to be obeyed* if you are to get through the jungle facing you. Finally, a functioning and creative imagination will cause the obstacles along the way to be solved one-by-one as you pass them. As you go forward, keep an eye out for the deeper meaning of the jungle travel and redraw your mind map in leadership strength.

HOW TO WALK THROUGH A JUNGLE

We lived in the deep inland jungles of Liberia sixty-five miles from the nearest road, so the only way to get to the African village and the mission where we lived was either to walk or fly! It was mentally and physically exhausting to walk through the jungle, and virtually impossible for a child to live while traveling through one. The sultry steamy deep jungles of West Africa are thickly grown together and impassable! A real jungle is where the trees, rope-like vines, huge leaves of vegetation, and thick underbrush literally cover the entire country. And the thick jungle is teeming with live animals. Because we could not walk through the jungle, we had a small airplane.

Years before us, however, Pauline Gruse, a single woman, had walked through the jungle with help from the natives, looking for villages to help. There were no maps for her to follow, only the faint trails that would become quickly overgrown by the jungle because of little usage. But Pauline's mind map was drawn to find people in need. Those who walked with her did not understand fully her purpose, only that she needed their ability and feet to navigate the jungle. At times, they literally would crawl up the mountainsides, holding onto bushes, vines, and tree trunks. She hated it, but she did it anyway because her mind map and her heart for the journey were stronger than her feet.

To walk through a jungle requires having a machete or ax because, with every step taken, something has to be cut out of the way, sometimes while branches, vines, and spiderwebs are all touching parts of you. Chop…chop…chop…. You pull the foliage down, then step or often climb over it to the next step. In the humidity, any kind of physical exertion will be exhausting in minutes. So a constant supply of water must be on hand to prevent serious dehydration.

Wild animals are a constant threat, and their numbers range from large fierce cats prowling around constantly to ground-hugging deadly spiders and bugs. And the many, many snakes that hang from the trees, looking just like vines! Keeping one's eyes open to what is around can mean life or death. Being conscious of one's surroundings matters most.

What you planned on eating for the entire trip has to be carried, so food and water for the journey is minimal. In some places, villagers will be willing to share food with you; in other places, people are more hostile. So food is saved for those times when it is safer to provide for one's own team. Plan to travel from sun up to sundown, as safety matters first in this wild place and reserving strength is crucial in the jungle.

USING THE MIND MAPS OF OTHERS

Finding a path already cut will only lead to one place in the jungle; it's not a mapped way to find any place else. The small narrow African trails are followed carefully by the locals who know the way to and from area villages. Yet even these paths become quickly overgrown by the aggressive jungle without regular use. Not many people venture out of their safe world to advance ahead. To cut a fresh trail requires stamina and courage to say the least. There are no maps to give out— only paid guides, who from their years of traveling, know where they are from the maps in their minds. These men are valued in a village because they can take a person from where he lives to where he wants to go. And there are no restrooms—only very watchful, quick private moments off to the side behind trees.

Your leadership road can be just like this…. It may be only a map to go by in your heart and mind. Uncharted "jungle" to cross day-by-day while you explore new territories and areas to work in. Leading your family is being done day-by-day by the mind map in your head. The goals you want to reach in life also will be carved out by your mind map.

Very few roads had been made into the interior and the few that existed were just dirt roads, so traveling from one place to another was very difficult for my family in Liberia. One trip could be costly in stripped gears, broken axles, burst tires, or a blown engine. Provisions and careful planning went into traveling by road; there were no gas stations with helpful owners for the traveler who found himself in difficulty. So all sorts of tools always traveled with one; tools were more important than a suitcase of personal belongings on the roads in Africa.

BRIDGE BUILDERS

We lived a humble life, across a rugged bridge from the actual village to show respect to the village of around seven hundred people. This was a roughhewn bridge made out of the chopped branches of trees laid down and held together with wire and a few nails. It was shaky, and each step taken was watched carefully since the rounded tree limbs were not steady or firmly in place. No risk could be taken of a possible fall into the river. Although in the past, other leaders had fallen into the contaminated waters to their disgust and the Africans' enjoyment.

Other bridges were known as monkey bridges, made of rattan vines and twisted into ropes that could be crossed high above the water. The higher the bridge, the easier it was to fall from. Learning how to walk on these bridges over the streams was an art. The smaller children would be carried over in the arms of strong Africans.

Once a flood swept away the bridge, and it had to be rebuilt by people risking their lives to enter the water. *But those who risk their lives to build bridges prove to be leaders worth following.* While that bridge had no handrails to hold onto, it was our lifeline to other human beings in a past world, and unknown to them, the bridge was their lifeline to a future world.

In many ways the tough environment, the hot climate, and the lack of nutritious food and education all played a part in the villagers' inertness in understanding to follow our mapped leadership into a better life.

Being a bridge builder is a gift of leadership. Finding a way to communicate to someone of different values, culture, and beliefs is how leaders teach others.

The easiest form of travel for us was flying, but it passed over the lives on the ground. For leaders to be effective, we can't always do things the easiest way; that puts us above the heads of those we are trying to lead. Often it is the tedious day-by-day walking beside—sometimes in front and sometimes behind—others in our work and faith that makes our mind map crystal clear to follow.

ON A WING AND A PRAYER

My father was a newly trained airplane pilot, and his first plane was a red and white, four-place Tri-Pacer, a very small plane. Transportation meant learning where we were at and going to while flying in the air. With very few instruments to fly by, Dad was always very careful. Flying was the quickest way for us to accomplish as much as possible and to get supplies. I remember that during each trip, Dad would check all the mechanical parts himself. And when we were loaded up, we would taxi down to the end of the dirt runway and turn the little plane around and stop. With the engines running, Dad would pray for our safety and flight. I would always feel the seriousness of his prayers, and the assurance that all would be okay, as I was sure angelic help was in the tiny plane with us. Six of us would be in that tiny plane, with two kids always on the floor, and only God knows how many angels flew with us each time!

Without a lot of instruments, Dad learned to fly by sight over the mountains, following the map of winding rivers below. When the mind map in your head charts the road map on the ground, traveling through life, work, love, and faith as a leader gets easier.

During our years in Africa, my father crashed two planes and miraculously walked out alive both times. Once, captured as an American spy, it took some time for him to get back to us in the jungle. I believe those little prayers at the end of the runway each time were the greatest prayers he ever prayed.

Lesson learned: The "easier" travel sometimes is the costliest.

MAPPING A PATH FOR OTHERS

Most natives were born, lived, and died in the same small village, having never known of an outside world. And except for the occasional brave hunter and adventuresome men, they all lived cloistered in their own small lives. The witch doctors would travel between villages on their own sets of paths, keeping the people bowed under their forms of intimidation and fear. These men kept the people tightly bound in terror, afraid to step outside of the boundaries set by their curses and demonic activity. And so education and learning were not possible for them. No one would change this from the inside. They were locked inside the jungle from their own fears.

CARRYING THE NEXT GENERATION

Coming home from church services in the village, I remember being carried in the darkness. We all would be in single file, walking; the leader would have the first flashlight, which he constantly shined around on the ground and up in the dark trees as we passed. The native carrying me would be walking behind my father, and others, with the flashlights' beams always flashing back and forth, would follow behind us. Stopping every so often to adjust my weight on his back, the native would continue on, humming. And then the whole train of people would start up again and we would continue walking until someone else carrying a child would need to adjust his or her load. Faithful followers carried the accordion, guitar, and the Bibles. Being carried on a native's strong back with my arms wrapped tightly around his neck always made me feel safer. I thought something in the tall trees would fall on me, so I was glad to be with someone who would protect me from it. Often the group would sing to keep the wild animals at bay and to keep our own thoughts of darkness and fear under control.

I think my brothers and I were all carried for safety reasons—not that we couldn't walk! But the Africans were kind and gentle, and they felt important and needed by carrying four sleepy children back to their mission, across the rugged bridge. Hearing them sing was soothing and enjoyable, even though it was in an African dialect I did not understand.

Some nights there were dark skies; other nights we had a bright moon; it was all amazing now that I think back to it. The one consistent thing we had, no matter how we traveled day or night, was the mind map in my father's head. My father's mind map was so powerful that he braved the dark, the lack of language, the jungle, animals, and the responsibility of his four kids to follow it. His mind map did not just lead him; it led the minds of the next generation in that nightly train.

CONNECTING WITH OTHER PEOPLE'S MAPS

Sometimes, it's not a road you need, or a plane to fly overhead; sometimes it's a connection with someone else who has been through the "jungle" ahead of you that's necessary. Once, there was a great need for help from the outside world for the orphans of Communist-controlled Romania. Right before the holidays one year, I was presented with a serious need. We were shown hundreds of orphans who were locked in concrete cells without food, water, or any toilet facilities. Not even the basics of human care were given to them. They were cold and broken little lost lives living in utter misery. The smuggled out pictures of them were shocking. I knew there had to be *something* that could be done.

As compassionate leaders, it becomes our responsibility to help whenever possible when the need is made known to us. Sometimes it's the reality of the need that drives our involvement to change something and create a map with which to effect change. *The past difficulties a leader has already forged through will build such a wall of determination that obstacles become only the latest challenges to conquer.*

So we planned a six-week long retail store in a mall for the coming holiday season to raise a substantial amount of cash to use for our project The Romanian Orphans. By selling lamps and small gifts, we raised the funds we needed in record time.

But we didn't have any contact with anyone who lived in Romania. The question haunted me, "How am I supposed to get supplies into a country I've never been to, and I don't even know anyone there?" Perseverance had already taught my husband and I through past lessons that it was time to watch and wait for the right person to come into our lives.

LITTLE MAPS STILL GIVE DIRECTION

Experience teaches us that watching for small doors to open is usually the path to pursue, but distraction will often keep you from watching for the still small opening. After the holidays, we traveled to California on our speaking tour; one night we mentioned to the crowd our plans to help the Romanian children.

Afterwards, a gentleman from Romania presented himself to us. He was planning to go there himself within the month. How did it happen that we were at the same place as he was on the same night? As my husband says, *"Right place, right time, every time."* The connection was made; subsequently, several important trips to Romania were made. Pressure was put on ashamed officials to change how children were being treated, and the children were fed and their living conditions drastically changed. Today, that same gentleman operates several orphanages himself in Romania. *Never underestimate the power of small things or the power of passion.*

TRAVELING A ROAD LESS TRAVELED

Why go through the efforts of such hardship to help people? One single word…compassion. We felt compassion for these struggling people living so far away from the modern world. Perseverance through our hardships would bring them help and could only come into their world from outside people. And who would dare to go? It was God, who loved them and had mercy upon them, who sent them families to love them. The villagers never knew of our personal sacrifice or understood how we were risking our lives out of compassion to help them.

QUESTIONS TO PONDER:

1. In your own leadership style, how do you navigate difficulties? If you had to choose one way of handling going through a map-less area, would you choose:

   a. A friend to go with you

   b. Tools to work with

   c. Plenty of supplies to live off

We would always choose tools. A leader can make friends along the way and create favor with people to find supplies, but tools are the valued implements that could be used to help the map in our heads be created into a reality.

2. In three sentences, can you clearly write where your mind map wants to lead you in terms of your life, work, and/or faith?

_____

_____

_____

7

Uncovering Your Positives

The difference between perseverance and obstinacy is that one comes from a strong will, and the other from a strong won't.
— Henry Ward Beecher

BECOMING FLEXIBLE

Living with adjustments is part of every leader's life. And the leader who learns not to allow the twists and turns of life to upset him will sail past those who become frustrated and lose their focus because of a time-detaining event. Your ability to navigate uncharted directions for the good of others develops your leadership into maturity. Often, life has an amazing way of putting answers right under our noses, so close to us that we may overlook them as an added hassle.

Flexibility is the ability to adjust with grace to unplanned changes. The secret to true leadership is to stay on track mentally while having to make unwanted adjustments that ultimately cause a greater understanding day-by-day.

When my family went to Africa, we did not plan on much that happened to us. First, the huge human needs that surrounded us were completely unexpected. Our every day was filled with seeing hunger, sickness, and poverty. Second, we did not expect children to land on our doorstep for us to house, feed, and take care of. African parents would abandon their little children on our doorstep in the predawn light, thinking we could give their children a better life. Certainly, they thought we could feed the children better than they could.

Before you are a leader, success is all about growing yourself.
When you become a leader, success is all about growing others.
— Jack Welch

Over time, this problem became two dorms filled with different tribes of boys and girls. It was a growing number of children to be fed night and day. Clothing somehow had to be found for them; then there was lots of washing and cleaning up and watching over all these running boys and girls. Not to mention, my parents had four of their own strong-minded, little, wild children growing every day.

Many times, my parents' personal lives had to be forgotten in the busy focus of just trying to keep up with all these children who were starting to come alive with nutritious food and education every day!

Rules had to be put into place to keep control and order, to have every child show up dressed and in the same place at one time to eat, and not to lose any little ones who might wander toward the hungry jungle where eyes were always watching for a weak one. Flexibility now had to take over to manage the changing work day-to-day. My parents felt the pressure of being responsible with all these children and the pressure from the villagers, who were privately watching every detail for a sign of weakness to report back to the chief or the witchdoctor.

WHEN YOU CAN'T SAY "NO"

My parents were in Liberia to "work," but they could not because of all the starving people, and all the children under our feet, night and day. But who could tell a starving parent that his or her child could not stay and be fed? The surprising changes occurring at our little mission were that while we were focused on one area, a different one was growing right before our eyes.

Finding a way to say yes will often lead to a greater purpose in our quest to fulfill destiny.

We were never consulted before the children would arrive; they would just be sitting on the doorstep when we got up in the morning. No chance for changing the parents' decision; our decision had been made for us. So acquiescing to the sheer needs of people became a variable in reaching our goal, and doing so later proved to be the wisest principle of all! I only remember one set of parents coming to ask whether their child could live with us, and of course, none could say no.

Once when I was faced with a tough situation, I heard the words in my mind, *"Is it because you won't...or you can't?"* Finding my inner compass in my heart, I knew I had been struggling with an "I Won't." The issue really was not an "I Can't." I understood that being obstinate was like putting my brakes on while driving a car; perseverance kept my foot on the gas pedal and helped me to realize that I needed to turn my own strong will into a force to uncover my positives in the situation.

FINDING THE POINT TAKES TIME

As stated previously, we could not learn the twenty-seven different tribes' dialects and show any favoritism. The children who attended school learned to speak pidgin English, a mixture of English and their different tribal words, in no certain word order. But as these orphaned little ones slowly grew up, they learned to speak clear English, and our school taught them to read and write also. My parents were not schoolteachers; nor were they trained in having a orphanage, so they did the next best thing—the four Latta children and the African children all learned lessons together.

Many of these children had been abused by parents who had no concept of love. Many of them came with scars and skin issues up and down their bodies. Boys and girls had blinded eyes because their parents had punished them for some childish disobedience by tying them down and squeezing stinging hot pepper juice into their eyes. They only understood war and fighting, and playtime consisted of someone possibly getting really hurt. We were like heaven to these children; they didn't want to go back to their homes. They called my parents Mama Latta and Father Latta.

One positive change that came about was that my brothers and I were able to communicate with these children as they learned English. They would watch us intensely; at times, I just wanted them not to look at me anymore because the scrutiny was nonstop. But our every move was copied and our every word said back to us. Touching my hair was constant once they figured out I didn't want them to. These bright children quickly learned to mimic us and our American ways. Thus they found ways to reach us when we couldn't reach them.

They were the answer to Africa's need...the positive solution was found right on our own mission. The answer was in the dirty, raggedy little boy and girl distractions that we thought hindered us from the far horizon we were focused on. Right under our arms were the unruly, and at times, obstinate, iron-willed little leaders to whom we were feeding nutritious food and clean water. We were finding clothes for them and teaching them how to behave—educating them all the while they were growing up. They were the positive change for Liberia's future. It took years to uncover that secret; we couldn't see very clearly at the time. We were really there in the bush, taking care of and growing tomorrow's leadership.

USING POSITIVE EMOTIONS

These African children did not understand crying…and if it happened, they were quick to mock and despise the one crying. Tears were a sign of weakness among the boys, whose mindset was to become a great hunter or warrior. Even the girls didn't cry, choosing to bear suffering as if it were a merit badge. But laughter was one we all understood, so we laughed a lot together. These children had to be taught how to share good emotions, how to love, have compassion for others, and to care for others and property, along with learning English and reading and writing.

The older ones helped to take care of the younger ones, and they were responsible for the gardening and chicken yard. Together, we all grew and learned from one another, and Christianity was slowly shared without using many words.

Don't miss my point here: The misunderstanding of leadership is often to focus on the trouble, the hassle that keeps happening. When that trouble may be the very feature of what you are trying to do, create, or be in the long run. The old cliché is really true—sometimes we cannot see the trees because the forest is in the way.

FINDING THE WILL INSTEAD OF THE WON'T

The surprise of uncovering positive answers in what is irritating and seems to be hindering you can show you the completed picture down the road of life.

As adults, these children became the governmental authorities, shop-keepers, bankers, executives, teachers, ministers, and pastors of their own people across Liberia and other nations as well. Thus, in the end, these hungry and poor children multiplied our labor a thousand times over. Many of that village's children are now adults who can be found in the world's major cities as fine, upstanding citizens.

What looks like a problem is really only the answer showing up in work clothes!

Children are the world's greatest asset, yet its most ignored. Finding a child and changing his or her life for the better provides a better prepared human being for countless others whose lives that child will impact in his or her future. It's the positive surprise that comes out of changing the big picture for single individual lives.

If you close your eyes to facts, you will learn through accidents.
— African proverb

Are your own answers right beneath your eyes? Often, it takes looking at the realities in your life with a positive mind to uncover the future. Look again at the unplanned, unwanted facts in your life and see whether your answer might be coming to you through an accident! Proper assessments make positive solutions!

QUESTIONS TO PONDER:

1. What is *really* going on in my life, while I'm trying to bring my focus of what I am trying to do to the forefront? What am I overlooking?

_____

_____

_____

_____

2. Who can I help as a leader in my life, my work, and my faith if I seriously want to effect change in other circles of people?

_____

_____

_____

_____

3. What is my *won't*?

_____

_____

_____

_____

4. What is my *will*?

_____

_____

_____

_____

5. Am I ready to accept that being a leader is not just about growing my own leadership skills, but it's really about growing my skills so I can successfully grow other leaders?

_____

_____

_____

_____

8

Watching for Bugabugs

It used to be about trying to do something.
Now it's about trying to be someone.
— Margaret Thatcher

IT'S THE LITTLE THINGS THAT MATTER MOST

Your leadership is not about becoming someone who will be important one day or someone who will be successful in the eyes of others.
The world is filled with people who step on others to climb higher on
their own ladders of importance.

As all true, mature leaders know, the definition of a successful leader
is not one focused on self-service, but rather, one who serves others
for bigger purposes. Leadership is about helping others have a better way of life. It's about achieving a greater good for all. The trend
that exalts "self" comes crashing down when the bugabugs of selfish
motives become revealed to others. No one can follow a leader who

---

1 The bugabug is a termite in Africa. I use the term here as a play on the word "bugaboo"—
something that causes fear, often falsely.

believes his own propaganda. Others can detect that kind of bugabug ego while its possessor continues to boast of abilities and assets.

Many an excuse will arise to become "me" oriented again. But the true heart of a selfless leader will press on no matter the personal cost because the heart is now involved in the higher purpose of leading others into a better tomorrow for all.

One night, my parents, brothers, and I were invited to see a large leopard that had been hunted by the native men, speared, and brought to the village. Of course, we children wanted to see it. The natives had built a roaring fire, and we could see the blaze and hear it popping and snapping in the distance. Soon, they would cut the leopard up into various sections after skinning him, the most important parts for the most important people first, and then down to the least important person. The witch doctor would take the claws, the eyes, the heart, and genitals, and the chief would get the best cuts of meat—his choice. The villagers wanted us to see first which part we might want—what an honor this was to us. Everyone in the village would eat well that night and for the next few days. Dad requested the skin and we were given it...more about that later.

As soon as we got close enough, the magnificent, large leopard could be seen in the firelight. He was dead and tied up by his paws on a long pole. He had been carried that way out of the jungle into the village. He was a beautiful creature. I didn't know he was dead, just that he looked like he was looking at me. All of a sudden, a native picked me up slightly and pushed me over to fall on him. I was so scared! I just knew that leopard was going to jump up and eat me! Everybody laughed at the little blond girl struggling not to cry from sheer fright. But I had wanted to come so I knew better than to start crying. I stood there, shaking inside, but trying not to show it.

The flickering bright firelight finally convinced me that the animal was truly dead and couldn't hurt me. But I never forgot seeing this wild animal, nor the hunters with it in the strange light of the fire. They could see my fright well in the dim light, but I couldn't see the glee in their eyes at all. The atmosphere for them was victorious, but I could sense fear, darkness, blood thirst, adrenaline, and killing. Man had won over the wild beast with nothing but a spear.

How correct your view is depends on where you stand.

Others will put you in sticky situations at times, for various reasons of their own. Sometimes, it's for ego, sometimes to make a point, sometimes a bet with others. It may be for nothing; the leopard may already be dead. Stop stressing.

They gave us the skin, covered in salt to cure it. It was tacked up on the side of our house to dry, so I had to see it every time I went past it. I worked past my fear of it when I watched the ants swarm over it. The smell was terrible, but the skin was beautiful, so everyone put up with it. But in the end, the ants got it…and we let it go to the smallest ones who always win in the jungle, the maggots.

Stop stressing—the leopard may already be gone…. It was a bugabug leopard that tried to make me afraid when there was nothing really to it.

DEBUGGING SYSTEMS

Our long dirt airstrip was constantly surveyed for any signs of bug-abugs each day. These were large termites that created big tunnels underground and big hills of dirt often overnight. They would build a hill of dirt reaching at times to three or four feet tall. The airstrip had to be monitored constantly since the "bugabugs" could under-mine and dig huge holes overnight. Thus it caused many accidents

111

to the unsuspecting person who happened to step on the bugabugs' underground cavern, which would suddenly collapse under one's feet and cause him or her to fall and break a leg or arm.

Our airplane's wheel once hit one of these bugabug hills and caused a major accident and the loss of precious equipment. We learned the importance of making sure to be vigilant about watching out for these bugs. It was more important to check the ground than it was to check our faces every day.

Inspecting for what you expect will always provide smaller problems to solve day-by-day than waiting till a big problem happens, which takes time, effort, and expense to redo or fix. You will need to inspect your areas of leadership daily if you want to make sure the bugabugs of mistakes, faults, or excuses don't undermine your efforts in life, work, and faith.

PITFALLS OF LEADERSHIP

One night after our cooling baths, my brothers and I were sitting with our mother on a small couch and she was reading The Pilgrim's Progress to us by a kerosene lamp. My father was spending the night in another mission so we were alone that night. It was dark and we only had a kerosene lantern to see by. I was thirsty and asked my mom to get me a drink. She told me to go and get it by myself. I didn't want to go because it was dark, but I obeyed and went toward the back of our small mud-packed house.

I was barefoot and forgot the dangers of a dark thatch-roofed house with a bare floor. When I got to the end of the kitchen area, I felt something furry under my foot. I screamed and ran back to my mom, crying that I had stepped on something! This upset her and my brothers. She picked me up and looked at my foot but saw nothing.

My mother was terrified of bugs, and being alone with the children, she knew she would have to deal with it. Wanting to deny a bug could be in the house, she tried to settle me down and read again. But I refused to calm down; I insisted that there was something on the floor and she needed to "get it."

So we all got up, she picked up the lantern, and we walked toward the kitchen. None of us wanted to stay in the dark; we wanted to be with Mother in our fear. We were all clinging to her skirt and scared. I was still crying. When we reached the place where I said it was—there on the floor was a black, furry, tarantula spider! Bigger than my foot! Now my brothers started wailing with me!

My mother froze for a second, forced her fear down, and hurried past it to set us all on the kitchen table. Then she got the broom, and trembling, went to send it into eternity. There was no way that ugly beast would be spending the night in our small house, even though we all slept under mosquito netting, tightly tucked in. At first, Mom tentatively jabbed at it with the broom. The spider, angered now, jumped on the broom! Mother screamed, dropped the broom, and jumped on the table with us! Now she was afraid that it had bit me.

In West Africa, these large poisonous spiders must be respected. Another missionary had lost her baby to a tarantula bite because she had not tucked the mosquito netting tightly enough under the baby's crib.

Now we were all crying and praying at the top of our lungs, "Save us, Jesus!" One of the native women heard us from the dorm and came running. We pointed and she saw the monster. She smiled, got one of my father's boots from the bedroom, leaned over it, and killed it. Suddenly, all tension was gone and peace returned! We were saved!

But Mother and the African woman had to carry each one of us back to the couch—we wouldn't walk past the dead creature.

Now looking back at that event, I have such a vivid memory of my mother's beauty and courage. She never blamed my dad for leaving her alone in the jungle with four small children, sometimes for many days at a time. She accepted her position and with strength faced her own battles day-by-day. That night we conquered a dreaded foe, and with her heart pounding, Mother quickly put all our shoes on us and finished reading our chapter for the night. She never had to tell any of us to wear shoes after that! And she won a place among the African women's hearts because she showed them she needed their expertise that night.

I can only surmise that after tucking all of us in tightly that night, Mother must have felt very alone and afraid when she went to bed. Did she sleep? The pitfalls of leadership often lead through lonely ravines of fearful experiences. But we are the leaders, so there is no one to give the reins to who will drive us through this fear but us… so we have to drive on. Growing leaders are inspired by our motives and led by our hearts, but tormented at times by our fears. The bug-abugs of life can force us into corners of petrified terror, unless we take control, educate ourselves about our fears, and conquer our foes.

Looking back, we should have immediately started shouting to sound the alarm and then stayed safely on the table, Mom included, until help arrived. There was no real need for us to go into a full panic like we had. But we were all young growing leaders who hadn't pre-planned what to do if a bug came into the house. Once you know… you know.

I remember my childish heart saying, "Thank you, God, for not letting that spider bite me when I pushed him down on the floor with my foot!"

It's your "need" that brings openness to building relationships, not your strength.

Judge not your beauty by the number of people who look at you,
but rather by the number of people who smile at you.
— African Proverb

From then on, the native women would smile at me…I didn't know the reason until I knew the proverb. When you know…you know. It was a bugabug of innermost fears that tried to undermine our confidence that we could take care of ourselves in the jungle. Instead, it showed us that we would find help when we needed it.

LOVE FORGETS ITSELF

In 1980, my husband and I were traveling the length and the breath of South Africa in our little travel trailer, car, and a motorcycle. We spoke in different churches, township halls, and schools. We, as a young white couple, traveled among all groups of people, but in those days, apartheid was alive and well. Racial segregation was very difficult and unwieldy to us as Americans who had Africans, Indians, and whites as our friends. Some could go with us only to certain places while others were limited in certain places, and yet our white friends could go anywhere with us. Each race had its laws and rules that had to be followed. We found it ridiculous and often verbally told people so.

These two outspoken young Americans were accepted with open arms by people of all different cultures, but shunned by the few who were still locked in their traditions. The day we found out in Cape

Town, South Africa that we were expecting a baby was both the happiest and the scariest day for us. Now all of a sudden, things were going to have to change. No more motorcycle rides for me, and we had to decide what would be best for the baby now coming. Before we could do anything, the Cape Town riots broke out in the area where we were staying, so we had to remain locked inside with a lot of time to think. Now what? Go home? Stay here?

Ultimately, we decided to stay in Africa, even though war was soon to break out in South Africa, and Rhodesia was already in a war to force its independence. The expected voices said in caution, you really should go back to the United States. But the unexpected voices said our baby will live the life we are living with us. We are staying. It proved to be unconventional, but the right choice since our friends from all cultures saw that we were serious and willing to risk our lives alongside theirs. Our love for them won out over our fears for our own lives.

The social and political bugabugs had eaten through every community and moral fiber, ruining the futures of millions with their apartheid rule. It had to change, and we stayed to see it all happen for those we loved in that nation. Our relationships remained strong with every culture as we determined to show what we felt should be as the regime was slowly forced into change. As a leader, you will be called upon to stand up for what is right and to be an inspiration to those who are struggling to overcome the undermining actions of controlling counterparts.

A true leader does not run from those he is leading; rather, he stays in the fray with them, thus leading them to victory every time. Often unconventional wisdom proves to be the unusual path a true leader will follow. I'm so glad we stayed...our daughter was born a Zimbabwean forever, bonding us to that land and its people through the earth-shaking war. And our actions proved that we would stand shoulder-to-shoulder and watch out for the bugabugs with the people because no one deserved to fall into the pits dug by self-serving leaders. We didn't know we were leading; we just wanted to be doing something good for the nation at war. It would be many years before we understood that our role had helped as young leaders in that great land.

Fears are felt by all, but only a leader will take charge, pushing back his own fears to bring calm to all. You are that leader who can do just that. It's not the big issues that often cause chaos; it can start with little things. Your experiences give you growing lessons in how to help someone else in need. Learning about the bugabugs in life will help safeguard a growing leader.

QUESTIONS TO PONDER:

1. What are you stressing over that remains alive in your mind, but already dead in other people's minds?

_____

_____

_____

_____

2. What system do you need to maintain daily and de-bugabug to keep your operating business running smoothly?

_____

_____

_____

_____

3. In the pitfalls of leadership, whom do you respect for what they have done for you?

_____

_____

_____

_____

4. And how do you remain true to them?

_____

_____

_____

_____

9

Discovering Unusual Friendships

In the moment of crisis, the wise build bridges
and the foolish build dams.
— *African Proverb*

DIFFERENT IS GOOD

As a leader grows, expectations change. You can learn to appreciate that things don't have to remain the same as in the past to be enjoyed. As a leader, you can allow different types of familiarities to be changed in your life, and you can reach out in new ways to people around you. Expecting the unexpected always brings wisdom through the many unusual people who enter a leader's life. Accepting those different characters brings humor and positive fun into life.

We had lots of unusual friends, my brothers more than I, but I did have a native friend, a little girl named Jatoo, who didn't know her age and spoke very little pidgin English. We were two little girls living in different worlds who could not communicate at all. Mother made us dresses to match for a special day. She was fierce...I was shy.

But Mother wanted us to look alike in our dresses. So we stood in our matching little dresses and silently looked at each other.

Once, my fine blond hair was woven by a native woman into tiny braids to look like Jatoo's hair. It didn't work, and I ended up being the laughingstock of the mission and village. They thought my braids looked funny, and I was embarrassed that I looked so bald while my friend's dark hair looked just fine. My mother called us friends, but the only thing we had in common was our growling stomachs each day. I wonder whether Jatoo remembers me like I remember her.... Mother tried to build a bridge between us, but it helped the mothers to bond more than the daughters.

Alan had native boys whom he played with every day. He still tells a story of how they taught him a lesson about leadership:

"Do not fish here!" the villagers angrily told us. "This is where our ancestors live." I was puzzled by these words until it was explained to me that these people believed their deceased relatives had come back from the dead to live as catfish in that part of the stream. Not to be deterred, my African friends tried fishing again a short distance downstream. To my amazement, we were left alone to enjoy our afternoon pastime even though we were sure that those same "protected catfish" could swim to where we might be able to catch them.

As a nine year old, I learned from these older youths that rath er than mocking, disrespecting, and arguing with adults whom we thought were silly and superstitious, we simply made their requested adjustment and still got to fish a short distance away.

Interesting encounters like this were mine to enjoy in the rain-forest when each Saturday, some of the students would take me fishing with them. Using cane poles, hooks, and hard crusts of bread, we would usually catch a catfish or two in the muddy water that separated the village from our mission, just as we did on that particular day when we were told where not to fish.

Walking through dense jungle to find better places to drop our lines was like a wonderland experience for this young white kid. Sensing new smells and strange sounds—as well as enjoying the cooler temperatures from the shade of the thick green canopy overhead—far outweighed any fear of venomous vipers, biting bugs, or leopards. Dodging saw-grass that could scratch like a knife, my friends—swinging sharp blades—would often cut trails from the vegetation that never seemed to stop growing, trying to reclaim its cleared places.

When we were thirsty, they knew just the vine to cut down that would provide cool water that was safe for this American boy to drink. Cutting more than we needed, this vine could be bent and tied like an archery bow to be carried as a natural canteen—string side up to keep the water from spilling out—so that we could have another drink later. Such fascinating things were learned from my new African buddies who knew how to enjoy the jungle.

I will never forget those boys who had moved to the mission—to better themselves with an education that was not available in their villages. While they were learning from the adults during the week, this American boy was learning from them on the weekends.

Just as showing some respect that day in the jungle—by quietly granting the wishes of the grownups we believed were being superstitious—still allowed us to catch fish, I learned that being patient with the perceived weaknesses of others allows us still

121

to be blessed in the long run. In this simple leadership lesson with unusual friends, I found a leadership principle that speaks of kindness and showing respect to others. Romans 12:18 says, "As much as depends on you, live peaceably with all men."

INNATE FRIENDS

One birthday, Mother made a present for me—a sock doll called, "Sunbonnet Penny Sue," made out of one of my dad's socks. She tried her best to make it special for me, but as a child, I knew my dad would go without one of his very small supply of socks for me. Funny how I remember that doll more than any other birthday present. It was a dark sock with two button eyes and a little white-stitched, crooked, smiling mouth. Its clothes were bits and scraps of cloth taken from the inside seams of other garments.

I don't remember ever playing with this doll because somehow I realized the sacrifice made to make her for me. I didn't want something to happen to her. Sunbonnet Penny Sue was my only birthday present that year…and she was a bridge to carry me past the "American" form of presents and into a new realm where presents had names and specialties appointed to them, so she was too precious to play with. Yet she was made to be so special in my eyes that she is the doll I remember from Africa. She was an inanimate object that was filled with love for me.

Books were another inanimate object that helped bring balance to awkward times. Still today, my library has familiar old friends, and I treasure the wisdom I have learned from them over the years. *The Pilgrim's Progress* was the imprint of the jungle season of life…another innate object that shaped a child's mind with leadership principles.

PETS AS FRIENDS

On a particularly hot sticky day, a hunter shot a large monkey for dinner. Upon picking up the dead female, he discovered she was pregnant with twins! So he did a surgery right there in the jungle and delivered two live baby monkeys. Then when he came back to the village, he walked over to the mission and presented us with the babies for a gift. We children were delighted!

One of the babies did not live long, but the other thrived and we all loved him. His name was "Monkey" and we all carried him around night and day. We adored Monkey and taught him to do many things—except become potty trained! He refused to learn. But he was an exceptional monkey that provided hours and hours of entertainment for four little children in the African jungle.

Between four children to carry him, Monkey never had to walk around very much. Usually, he was hanging on someone's shirt, his legs wrapped around the child's waist, and holding onto the shirt collar with his one arm pulling it out of shape continually. Mother fussed, but Monkey still did it. And we let him. He would suck on our earlobes and we would laugh so hard; Mother fussed, but we let him do it anyway.

Monkey was always inquisitive. He would try anything, and he was so smart that we only had to show him something a few times and he would be trying to do the same trick. One time, a friendly native brought us a whole stalk of bananas. It was such a thoughtful gift, and we were all really looking forward to having fresh ripened bananas for a couple of weeks.

A couple of days later, we left the mission and went across the bridge to the village church for a church service. (Mom and Dad refused to let Monkey go to church with us, although we begged and begged.)

Monkey was so mad that he wasn't going; we left him shrieking on the screen door. So he decided he would make sure that no one would eat any of the bananas. He took all of them off the long stalk and piled them on the seats of the chairs around our table. And as he stacked them up, he took a big bite out of each one! He knew our mother would not let us eat anything that he had already bitten into!

When we came home, we did not suspect anything until we went to sit down at the table to eat the next day! Everyone was so surprised when one-by-one, we pulled out our chairs and found his revenge. We all laughed and laughed at him!

Another time when we left him alone, he picked up a large gallon jar of pickles (a very, very rare luxury for us, and one we were saving for a special occasion), wrapped his arms around it, and carried it to the floor, trying to get the lid off. Finding that impossible, he did the next best thing—open it from the bottom. Now this made perfect sense in his little monkey brain. He simply picked it up and dropped it hard, breaking out the bottom of the glass jar.

When we returned, he was sitting in the pickle juice, happily eating pickles. A big pickle smile spread across his face and his fur was completely soaked from his pickle party fun! This time, all of us children giggled quietly, hoping Mom did not see our secret smiles.

Monkey grinned at us and we grinned back behind Mom's back. As she rushed to get him out of the house and the four of us away from the broken glass, he was reaching for us with his little green pickle hands. We did not dare go to his rescue this time—Mom meant business!

He loved us and we adored him! He took turns with each of us, staying with only one child until that one had something better to do, and then he would find another. He was the most entertaining monkey in Africa. He could wear Barbie clothes and play Barbies with me, then become G.I. Joe with one of the boys and ride in their little jeep (just his size), then catch a ball with another, and sneak a snack with another child. And back again. Life was a grand fun event for him!

Different animal friends brought us various kinds of joy. We had an anteater friend named Pinkie, whom we loved putting in the bathtub with us. Our animal friends usually didn't last long, however; often they would turn up missing, having been eaten by some passing hungry creature. We had a tabby cat that was bitten by some wild thing; she got away only to become terribly infected and we weren't allowed to be around her again. Our little kitten, Sunshine, had to be shot because she contracted rabies somehow.

Someone finally got smart and fashioned a collar with big spikes around it for our pet dog. The collar would prevent him from getting squeezed and eaten by the huge and hungry boa constrictors in the jungle. A boa constrictor did come around once that was over twenty-feet long. We didn't want him for a pet; he was big enough to eat a small child! But we learned to love the pet that was in front of us and live in the moment of joy with it. Our pets were better than any television entertainment could ever be, and they promoted healthy mental attitudes for us every day.

A child can learn leadership principles from having an animal to take care of. And the reality of life and death for our pets helped us to understand the fragility of life itself. We were never bored, nor got into serious trouble, because we had animals to care for.

QUESTIONS TO PONDER:

1. Learning that different is good can help you as a leader to step outside the norm and look at unusual friends to gain new perspectives in life. Who is that unusual friend you have learned from?

_____

_____

_____

_____

2. Have you ever had a pet teach you a leadership principle? If so what was it?

_____

_____

_____

_____

10

Activating Communication and Coordination

If your mouth turns into a knife, it will cut off your lips.
— African Proverb

THE OUTSIDE WORLD

An unusual friend can come into your life to help keep your perspective sane. Sometimes the strangest characters will help you overcome the rocky loneliness of leadership. And how you choose to let them into your life can bring humor and an easing of the pressure that you feel at times.

Learning to communicate was critical in our lives, and coordinating with each other was a daily action. Everyone knew where everyone else was all the time. In the bush, my dad had a generator set up, and once a day at 4:30 p.m. when he was with us, he would crank it up and sit down to talk on the radio. It was a pre-arranged time for all the missionaries to talk to each other from across the country in different African villages.

Each missionary from different church denominations checked on the other ones, making sure everyone was okay—no one was sick, hurt, wounded, or in need. I remember Dad talking about fuel needs, money situations, and when we could get together for some fellowship. They would share any news from home or political news from the land in which we were all living. At times, each leader suffered from being homesick and needed to hear a voice over the radio that was assuring and encouraging. No one in the world but they themselves knew what these weary leaders went through, but across this little nation, they connected day-by-day through their shortwave conversations called ham radio.

Time was so short, so precious calls were not spent on complaining or gossip, but simply the positive supportive words that encouraged each one to continue on in his or her jungle missions. They coordinated with each other about supplies and sharing what anyone had to give who was in need. Everybody knew the high price of leadership each was paying. So communications were uplifting and tried to bring constructive messages to all who were listening.

The day my dad crashed his plane and disappeared for days, my mother and we children were alone in the bush with the native villagers and the mission children. I remember Mother figuring out how to turn the generator on and then going to the radio and calling out for any news about Sam Latta. Neither Dad nor she had taken the time for her to learn how exactly to handle the ham radio system, so she had to learn by herself now when it was most important. She had simply trusted Dad, but now she wished she had taken the time to learn.

There was silence over the radio.... It was not the arranged time for the missionaries to be on the radio. She called over and over, looking for anyone who had any news about him. I heard someone in English ask for anyone who might know where she could get diapers for her newborn child. It was another missionary from a different denomination. But no one had heard about my dad's plane going down.

So we waited. Mother was quiet, just trusting that God knew where she and the children were, and even where Dad was. Each day, she tried at different times to connect with the outside world. She didn't say a concerning word about being in the jungle alone with four children. I'm sure she was deeply worried, but she never spoke it or infected us with fear. And then after several days, someone had news on the radio and told us Dad was alive and safe and sound. We could have kissed that old radio that day! Mother's persevering efforts to communicate and coordinate had finally caught up with someone who had heard that Dad had crashed the plane.

The value of communication and coordination kept our lives stable after long days of struggle to communicate with tribal people. My dad finally came back and kept that old ham radio in top order. Sometimes, he could get on it at night and hit the "skip" zone to talk to the United States; it was always the best nights when that happened. It was an entertaining break from the dead silence and smoky jungle heat. Just talking to strangers who spoke English helped to pass the lonely nighttime hours tucked far away in the African jungle.

In this day of modern technology, satellites, and mobile phones, we don't even think about how hard it used to be to talk to someone across the world. Today, it's as easy as pressing the country code and phone numbers from wherever you are. And all this has transpired in my lifetime! Amazing!

The villages communicated with each other through drums; loud and deep barreling sounds would pour out news of deaths, attacks, and witchcraft. Once, the drums beat in our village night and day for three days without stopping. And as a child, I clearly remember the oppressive and heavy feeling we all had as a result of that loud sound that could not be shut out. While it was the villagers' way to send their message and we heard it loud and clear, we did not understand the message.

It truly was a giant step for mankind the day man stepped foot on the moon! No one could possibly understand how that momentous event would jump the world ahead in communication. We were in Africa when it occurred, and there was no way to get the people to understand our nation had just landed on the moon. They just laughed us to scorn. In some ways, it seemed like we lived on two different planets at times.

How does one tell someone who lives in another world about technology and its modern advancements around the world? These people had no concept of telephones, televisions, cameras, or even electricity. Those were all "white man" issues, and they didn't concern themselves with such "lies." Their educational, traditional, and cultural background was vastly different.

So instead of taking them into our world, we had to learn to go into theirs. Leadership requires that those who are leading do not get so far ahead of the followers that the followers lose sight of the leader. But rather, the leader must pace himself to the followers' understanding to take them where he is going.

We laugh together today about trying to teach the natives the song called "The Royal Telephone." This old English song was about the ability to pray and reach God as if using the telephone. At times, what our communication and coordination failed to teach the Africans was made up for in the humor for us kids! Watching the villagers' faces turn in questioning, bewildered looks was enough to make us start giggling together every time! That wasn't helpful to our dad, who was trying to teach them with four unruly kids watching.

SEEING THE BIG PICTURE

One time, we were invited to attend a special celebration of America's Independence Day at the American Embassy in Monrovia. My entire family was excited to get to see and talk to some Americans for a real break.

When we arrived, a live band was playing happy American music, and bright picnic tables were set up on the lawn all dressed up in red, white, and blue tablecloths. The American Ambassador served *real American hot dogs with American mustard and American catsup and American pickles and real American potato chips!* We were treated to special anthems and speeches, and all Americans who were serving for various reasons in that African nation were honored and treated so well by our government.

And at the end...*real American ice cream*...as much as we wanted to eat! It was thrilling to us children to eat to our hearts' content and not have to split pieces or take only one or share with each other.

And when it got dark...*fireworks with music!*

I was enthralled—it was my first time recognizing that America was an awesome country and I was proud to be a little American...a day of firsts for me. We hadn't had American food in such a long time, and it made a deep impression on me. Even as a child, I felt that our government knew my family was alive and trying to help Africans.

We felt the government's support that day, and it left a lasting mark... of the bigger picture of all the good that our nation was doing to help the world's people. We were encouraged to keep trying, keep bringing aid, to keep teaching, to keep loving, and never to give up on our separate missions to help people. The principle of positive words can be used to inspire the hearts of the weary, the discouraged, and the lonely.

Powerful words can propel men back to work in the same environment, with nothing changed but a different mindset.

We were encouraged to communicate and coordinate with all other Americans in Liberia. And wisely, the government had put together an event that allowed all of us to come together to meet. Leadership does that—it connects people for the good of others, not necessarily for the good of self. The embassy's bigger cause was to serve each family serving the nation. And our bigger cause was changing lives, altogether like one team that works together. Each of us was accomplishing great things that were adding up to a bigger purpose and a greater good for all.

The ambassadors who serve Americans around the world are needed and appreciated by each family that lives in a nation in need. We were given the opportunity to talk with the ambassador and ask questions; even as a child, I recognized the value and unity of each family standing together, all being encouraged in their work.

Funny how the power of familiar food always makes one feel more at home. And a pat on the back causes each person to want to do more. We left that day feeling ten feet tall, and ready to go back and do better work, be more understanding, and give of ourselves in a greater measure.

Communication does not require coordination, but coordination requires communication. Many leaders communicate, but they fail to coordinate to make sure gaps don't occur. Clear instructions are invaluable to keep misunderstanding from happening. How do you keep your team focused if these two elements are not in use? A team cannot work well together without coordinating efforts. Our ambassador's efforts acknowledged the many sacrifices and crashes, dangerous treks, and going without ourselves for the good of humanity… and it helped.

STOPPING DISCOURAGEMENT IN OTHERS

Long after I was an adult and married, I found myself again serving and giving among the poor. Our personal sacrifices seemed ridiculed by our peers, who disdained the needs of those in poverty and excused themselves, believing it was someone else's responsibility to do something for the poor. This negative energy was draining to us and kept us pushing back doubt about the value of our work. While our peers rode around in fine cars and lived in big fancy houses, we were working to ship containers of food, clothing, medical supplies, and aid of all types to people in the nations we knew were suffering. Once, a person we knew told us, "You need to get yourselves a decent car," not understanding our purpose or goal to be a pipeline of supply for the developing world at large. His misunderstanding of our dream and purpose did affect us, and it was a disappointment to both of us.

Soon after one of these conflicting admonishments, we were honored as one of the One Thousand Points of Light. This was a huge encouragement to us. We were invited to Air Force One to meet the President of the United States of America, George H. W. Bush. President Bush came to us personally and put his arms around us both, looked us directly in the eyes, and said, "You kids are doing great work. Don't ever think what you are doing does not matter. It's important work and I am proud of you." He could never have known what his words did for us that day to affirm us and support us in our efforts and labor after the years we had struggled with negative influences around us. He commended us as #389 among the One Thousand Points of Light in America.

The president's friendship changed our paradigm as we realized we had just been in the wrong circle of people for support.

President Bush's leadership to us was a personal positive word that changed our minds about what others thought. I shall never forget his kindness—it helped so much. An invitation to join the President of the United States at Disney World thrilled our daughter and humbled us. Continuing till this day are the rewards of that unusual friendship.

When the needs around you become greater in your mind than the words of those who are watching, as a leader you will do something about those needs, no matter what. And in time, the unusual can step into your world and affirm what you have become known for. Different is good.

QUESTIONS TO PONDER:

1. What would you say is your greatest and strongest communication skill?

   _____

   _____

   _____

2. What is your weakest coordination skill?

   _____

   _____

   _____

3. Have you ever gone too far ahead of your team?

_____

_____

_____

4. What principle did you use to get the team's focus back on track?

_____

_____

_____

5. How important is it in your leadership team to communicate a positive message to your staff each time?

_____

_____

_____

6. As a leader, do you recognize the need to encourage those who are working beside you, and how do you support their efforts on a regular basis?

_____

_____

_____

7. Which of the two is your strongest ability? Communication or coordination?

_____

_____

_____

11

Identifying Your Coaches

Did Noah build the Ark, or did the Ark build Noah?
— Bishop Gregory Holley

TROUBLES THAT TRAIN

Throughout this book, you are seeing the trend of actual happenings transcending into principles of leadership. One must ask the right question, find the puzzle pieces, have courage enough to let go of comfortable lifestyles, and learn to adjust to a new reality with sacrifice and giving of self. The leader within you is developed through experiences, pressure, responsibility for others, and a mission to accomplish.

Developing leadership skills always causes variations in learning a new mind map to travel a different road, and discovering more adjustments for a bigger cause. The old Bible story of Noah building the Ark represents a leadership lesson: As Noah built the Ark, it was also the other way around—the Ark was building him. The extra headaches of planning details over and over, the people problems, all the many animals to gather, house, and feed, the lack of skilled workers, and the money issues all trained Noah how to rule in the washed earth when he again set foot on dry land.

Your ability as a leader is being shaped and trained by all of the personal life events you experience.

PAPER TIGERS

One night while my family was in the dimly lit village church, a leopard came prowling around outside the building. Dad was blazing away preaching when, suddenly, we heard Africans running around beating branches and yelling, with brushing sounds and growling sounds getting louder and louder. Banging noises began, so we thought maybe someone was trying to get some "spirit" to leave. My dad never stopped preaching but kept the service going, no matter what was happening outside. The commotion outside became louder than the service inside. Dad just raised his voice louder and kept on preaching! No one was listening to the service anymore; we all were nervously looking around, wondering what was happening outside, but being polite, the natives didn't want to walk outside to check.

Then we heard the snarling screams of an animal outside the door! We children all looked at our mother for assurance as Dad kept on marching around and preaching. She patted us and motioned for us to "Watch your father" and to be quiet. Then, suddenly, with a thump, everything calmed down outside and gradually the people settled back down. And the outside noises died as people walked away.

When the service was over and we all got up to leave the building, we discovered a grown leopard lying dead with a spear through him on the church doorstep. I didn't want to see him, having already had a bad experience with another leopard. But I tremble to think what might have happened if the natives hadn't been alert outside the building that night.

Many are those outside the circle of your friendship but inside your sphere of influence who help you.

Thank God they were outside that night and not inside. Here is a leadership secret: This was just a paper tiger to my dad; he never lost focus while speaking. Maybe at twenty-nine years old, he didn't know what to do, so he kept doing what he was doing when the commotion started. It was the best thing to do because if he had stopped and sent someone to check, or gone himself, there surely would have been a serious attack and a possible death that night. His wisdom to stay steady and keep going literally saved lives that night.

Following the leader's lead in a tense situation can prevent more drama from happening.

The leopard actually taught a leadership lesson that night: Never lose your focus in the middle of your mission because of distracting trouble. That leopard was a leadership coach to us all.

The unexpected will happen at times. Finding out that others will watch your back brings the knowledge that strong relationships with others will be as the small roots of a tree that will intertwine hearts, circumstance by circumstance, in life.

The wise leader will not forget what is done for him; he will remain true, giving back the same values. It is a pitfall of leadership to forget over time what has been done for us when we have been the recipient. The giver never forgets, but the recipient often does. And the paper tiger is always forgotten.

The Rhodesian War years, which lasted from 1964-1979, were hard ones of bloody warfare and thousands of terrible deaths on both sides of the conflict. After our baby was born and we lost all funding, my husband had to find work to support us. It was not easy to find funding or others to help because many were leaving the country as the war spread into the city where we lived. This was a time of shaky fear as day-by-day, no one knew who would be left alive by nighttime.

But this situation served as a personal coaching experience for us as we raised chickens, creating a chicken and rice restaurant that not only provided us with funds but also helped many hungry people. While bombs continued to go off in the downtown district, our little restaurant, also downtown, fed people night and day. We would raise the chickens in our church family's yards and then use the chickens as our supplies were needed. The chickens weren't worried about war, and it helped our families to have something good to talk about in the face of terror each day. So this enterprise seemed quite natural and provided a small sustainable income for us during that hard time. We had several coaches during that experience. The loss of funding was one—it taught us to think outside the box. We became caught in a war zone, which coached us to find ways to keep life normal. Our baby didn't have diapers, which coached us to find solutions not only for her but many others as well. The lack of security each day coached us to kiss each other goodbye each morning as if it would be the last time we saw each other alive. We appreciated each other tenderly.

WHO'S WATCHING WHO?

On a recent workday, our secretary called to tell us that we had special unexpected guests. The door opened and a entourage came in with Bishop Abel Tendekayi Muzorewa, the first Prime Minister of Zimbabwe. We both were so thrilled to see him...and in our own offices in America as well! We didn't know quite what to say...we had only watched him from afar in parades in Harare some thirty years ago!

How did he know us? And how did he find us? It was so humbling to see this elder African statesman walk into our world to speak with us. After we spoke for a while about Zimbabwe and the history of long ago, he told us the reason for his visit. He said, "Everybody noticed the two white American kids who traveled through our nation during the war. No one could miss the two of you! Gayla, you were pregnant, and Gregory, such a bold young man in the bush. I wanted to thank you personally before I died. Thank you for feeding my people…thank you for giving my people your clothing…thank you for your love…and thank you for your support for the people of Zimbabwe. Neither of you knew that you were feeding the freedom fighters when you would bring food to the people. No one touched you because of what you did to help us. Yes, you were in danger many times, but not from us…. We knew you believed in equality for all men by how you fed the people many times."

Tears flooded my face as he spoke. Truly, we never knew all of this; we had just innocently seen suffering people and wanted to ease their pain somehow.

We moved among the Rhodesian army, often riding on their army convoys throughout the nation to help the very people they were fighting. And on trains and buses with the people…no one ever touched us. In fact, we didn't think many times people even saw us! It was like we were invisible in the crowds of people. But while we were feeding the very ones fighting to end the injustice of the former system, they were watching over us.

It's amazing now to think that we rode in the Rhodesian army convoys of weapons, tanks, and helicopters, and we even held the army's guns in the vehicles. Once while holding the machine gun, which was the payment we had to agree to in order to ride with them, my husband was so tired he fell asleep with his head on the gun barrel with the gun standing up between his legs. The Army guys and I were too afraid to wake him because he might have accidentally pulled the trigger. We worked among all sides and were never touched by anyone for our humanitarian efforts.

As a growing leader, you may never know who is standing behind you...watching. And the life you save as a leader while offering compassionate aid may be your own. It does matter who you are, and what you do. For there are those driving by in the motorcades of power who are watching your efforts to help and will take note of you. The leadership lesson that day was of the overwhelming humble compassion of a great leader who was watching and took careful note of two nobodies alongside his people, and who remembered to come to America to say thank you...thirty years later.

The "Ark" you are building will someday carry you. The work and experiences are actually the coaches in your life helping you to grow into the next phase of development and leadership.

QUESTIONS TO PONDER:

1. Your troubles are training you for greatness. Can you list the lessons you have learned as a result of all that has happened to you?

_____

_____

_____

_____

2. What is the name of your Ark that you are building?

_____

_____

_____

_____

3. Can you articulate what your Ark has taught you for the new world you are building?

_____

_____

_____

_____

4. What has defeat trained you in?

_____

_____

_____

_____

5. Whom are you helping so that you don't care who is watching?

_____

_____

_____

_____

The Latta family the year my parents decided to go to Africa.

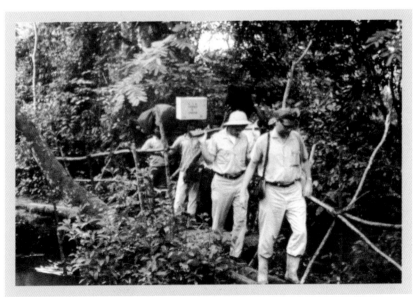

Traveling African style through the jungles of Liberia.

Landing strip in the jungle.

Fassama village where
we lived 65 miles from
the nearest road.

Fassama Bridge that
led to the village.
I was carried over
this bridge at night.

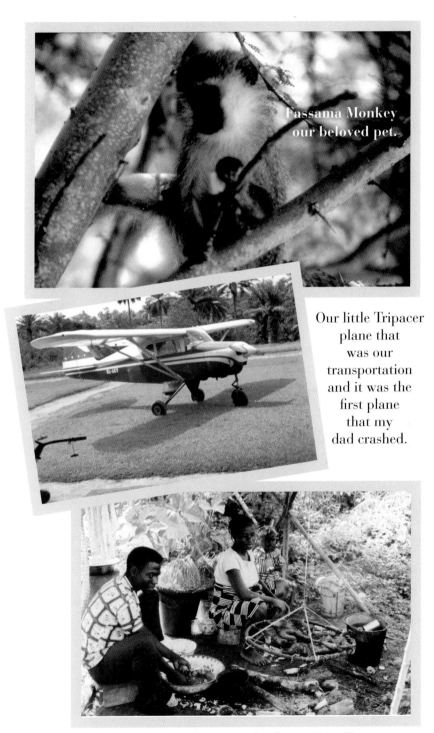

Fassama Monkey
our beloved pet.

Our little Tripacer
plane that
was our
transportation
and it was the
first plane
that my
dad crashed.

Cooking monkey over the fire in the village.

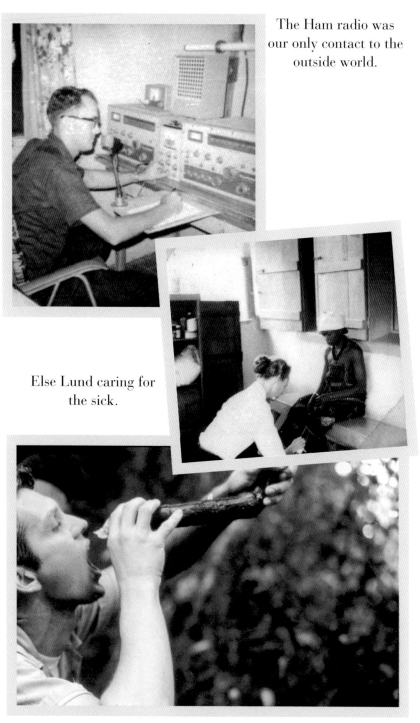

The Ham radio was our only contact to the outside world.

Else Lund caring for the sick.

Drinking pure water from a jungle vine.

Laverne's grave in the yard of the mission.

Pauline Gruse who walked in the jungles and
started the Fassama Mission.

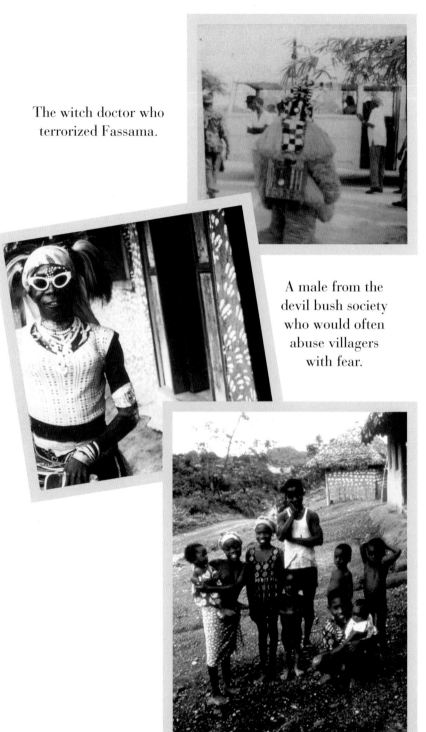

The witch doctor who terrorized Fassama.

A male from the devil bush society who would often abuse villagers with fear.

Fassama children

The passenger plane that crashed close to our home.

Mexico City feeding children who live in a landfill.

A mother delivers a baby after Hurricane Katrina while staying at our shelter.

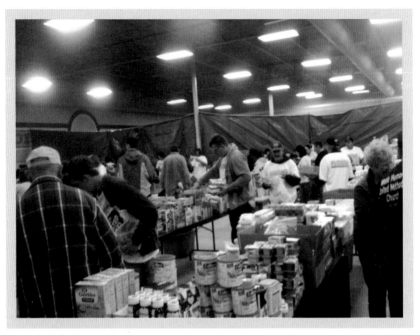

Serving the families in the American Midwest after
the deadly tornados.

A container of 250,000 meals is delivered to Fiji after the floods.

A children's hospital receives supplies.

A baby with cancer deserves to be loved.

Feeding children living in a swamp in Fiji.

Children at risk are fed nutritional meals.

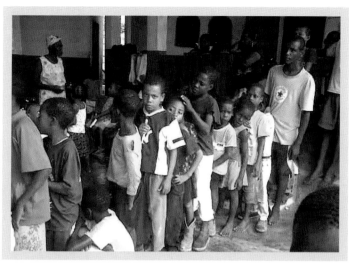

18 containers of food, medical supplies, clothing and aid are shipped to the children in Haiti.

Orphans in Haiti receive help.

A child begs in Guatemala.

Food shipments are sent to Guatemalan children.

The feet of a child in Guatemala.

Shipments are
prepared and sent
to developing world
countries with the
help of donations
from Mothers.

Church in
San Marcos
– Mothers in
Mexico help to
feed the needy
children in
small villages.

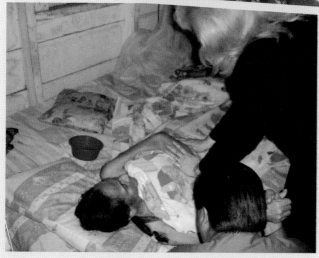

Guatemalan mothers receive care.

Ghana gratefully receives a container of 250,000 meals.

African mothers receive training.

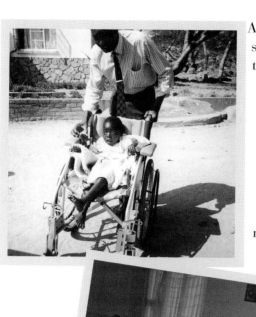

African handicapped child sits in a chair for the first time and not the ground.

Romanian orphans no longer live in squalor but have proper care and housing.

Latin American children are 4th highest in the world for chronic malnutrition.

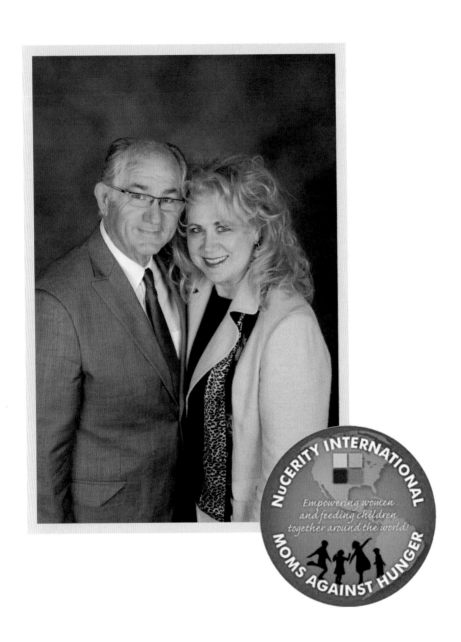

Bishop Gregory and Gayla Holley,
Nucerity and Moms Against Hunger work together
to save lives around the world.

12

Honoring Your Foundations

A family is like a forest...when you are outside, it is dense;
when you are inside, you see that each tree has its place.
— African Proverb

THOSE WHO HAVE GONE BEFORE US

You will agree with me that no one is entirely responsible for the leadership roles we play in life and work. It has been said that we are standing on the shoulders of those who have gone before us into the halls of history. All peoples are connected with each other somehow in the links of life. The old African proverb describes our family as being like a forest with each member being a tree. Each family member in his or her own way has added value, brought strength, given his or her talents to benefit the family, and together, everyone's capacities have formed the family. Each person is important and not to be forgotten, even after departing.

In your family tree, who are the outstanding ones who have built businesses or started brand new ideas that transpired into greater or easier ways for doing your work today? Without their foundations of hard work, you would not be where you are today. Or are you that person who now is standing in the place of leadership in your family tree and will change the direction and focus of your family? One day, others will stand on our shoulders, looking in the direction we have pointed them to see. How will your efforts today make that happen for them tomorrow? It is the long range view of leadership.

Often while driving from Texas to California across the mountains, I think of the men and women who faced all odds, all difficulties, many giving their very lives, to cross such life-threatening ridges to settle these remote areas. Being buried right alongside the trail they were traveling, these souls are the poignant heroes we now roll past in our rushed modern world. Their determination and stubborn grit made them invincible as leaders in the process, and eventually, some of them reached the lands of their dreams. We are all better people because of their abilities and work ethic.

But because of them, we are now at the juncture where we are standing. Their trees make up the foundation for our trees to flourish and grow. At some point, a family tree has to produce fruit...are you that fruit?

For Africans, their respect for their families is lifelong. Certain aspects of their deep esteem can be additionally beneficial to helping our family trees remain together. Sadly, the fragmentation of a real family is taking place in our society today; few honor the root system of their family unit anymore. A leader will guard the history of the family unit to preserve the longevity and promotion of its own people.

Liberia has a history of courageous leaders who built Liberian missions and schools far back in the jungle as early as the 1940s. A forest of trees called Mother Holmes, Pauline Gruse, Velda Russell, Ena

Hylton, Laverene Collins, Gladys Robinson, Porter Davis, the Parks family, the Basil Williams family, the Cupples family, the Davises, Else Lund, the Garlands, Mother Bailey, the Pettys, and the latest ones up to that point were the Lattas. These trees were planted in Liberia and lived rugged lives of leadership among the natives. Out of this list of mighty leaders, eight were single women. It's amazing that these women were brave enough to go alone to the jungles of Africa to fulfill their life callings. I stand on their shoulders.... How could I possibly not continue the work of giving compassionate care by their early examples?

WHEN THE TREE BECOMES LUMBER

Fassama is the burial place of one of God's special young women. Her name was Laverne Collins. She arrived a few years before us, and she had not been properly trained in the dangers of living deep in the tropics' jungles. Nor did she know about the dreaded malaria that is so easily contracted there through mosquitoes. She did not understand that her very life could be at stake unless she took precautions to protect her health. She taught school every day, and the Africans used to say her favorite word was "pretty." Beauty was something important to her, and this forty-two-year old woman found beauty in the harsh land she had chosen. She was very happy there and felt like her life was worthwhile in Fassama.

Unfortunately, she died six months after her arrival from what was believed to be cerebral malaria. The natives were disappointed and did not understand why she had come there only to die. Why had this occurred? But even missionaries live in human bodies and must take care with their health. They are not immune to sickness if they are uneducated about jungle life. Even leaders must use medical precautions.

147

The other single missionary woman with Laverne was Pauline Gruse, who tried to nurse her the best she could. Laverne's death was both trying and traumatic to Pauline, who was already struggling with terrible loneliness. She tells of sending a runner for help through the jungle, but it would take days for the news to reach Bomi Hills, the closest mission, so Jack Langham could come. It was a darkness that was felt by this lone woman in her sorrow. She buried Laverne in the yard outside her house and her little funeral was attended by Africans who said, "She was a stranger here.... We will show respect for her. At least she came...."

Laverne was honored by my father and mother when they arrived. My dad gave her a proper concrete burial plot with flowers. Her grave is still marked today, back in the jungles of Liberia, sixty-five miles deep into the bush. She was a leader...for at least she went when others did not. I remember my parents gathering us children and having a small memorial service there at her whitewashed grave. We sang a little song.... Dad gave a little message with just us there...two lone adults and four children standing around the little freshly painted white marked grave.

The reality of it all is that leadership is for keeps, not a game to be dropped when life gets hard or a fantasy to become "someone." *The real leader is one who is committed to a cause no matter what happens.*

Our parents told us about Laverne often, making sure we would take our medication every day for her sake—the hated quinine pills that render the malaria sickness harmless if bitten by a mosquito. We listened and tried to choke down that horrible bitter tasting pill every day because of Laverne.

Mother would melt the pill, mash it in jelly, try to mask it with juice, make us hold our breath, and swallow hard, all trying to get us to eat quinine. It is certainly the nastiest tasting medicine on the planet! But it kept us safe. We would cry and plead, "Not tonight, Mom," but she would remind us again of the whitewashed grave in the yard. We dreaded that ritual, but she would not give in, and we would somehow get the horrid thing down every night.

And Laverne, you did your part protecting our lives by educating us, as we did understand the sacrifice that you had made and the seriousness of the situation fighting mosquitoes. Four little kids may have survived while living deep in the heart of Africa thanks to your sacrifice.

Bonnie Laverne Collins 7/7/13—8/1/55

In Bomi Hills Mission was another grave, that of the Langhams' own teenage daughter, who was accidentally shot by a young African man. And there have been others who have laid down their lives in the call of duty.

Herein lies the reality of a leader's life. The leader is not someone who is perfect, whom none of life's tawdry smears has touched; rather it's one who *has* been through countless pains and sorrows—thus building a deep foundation of compassion for the needs of others. Our tree becomes lumber for the betterment of all, for building wisdom, for building selfless purposes, for building a better tomorrow.

WHEN A TREE BECOMES USEFUL

Pauline Gruse was an extraordinary leader. As an eleven-year-old girl, she desired to become a medical missionary, but it would be almost twenty-five years later, and through many heartbreaking seasons, before she followed her destiny. Prior to getting to that place of fulfillment, she experienced the long road of the struggle of training to become a nurse, going through the loss and suffering of two divorces,

149

giving up her only child to others, and then finally, her break came in life and she seized the moment.

This mighty "tree" of a woman spent twenty-eight years in Liberia, giving of herself as a true leader among some of the worst places to live on earth. Useful? Ultimately, she provided education, healthcare, and a spiritual awakening for thousands of lives.

She opened the Fassama Mission. She walked over death-defying mountains, facing resistance in the villages, supporting other leaders who could not keep up the pace with her. Eventually, she would leave them in different areas and continue on alone through the jungles with a guide. Once she walked through a river so deep that the water made her tip her head back not to drown. Was she afraid? Of course. But did she allow her fears to stop her? No.

Pauline had already twice had a broken heart from her divorces and having to let her only child go to family members before she got to Africa. She had been coached by the best trainers life could offer, and she did not allow anything to break her. Instead, she became highly trained in tough living, and eventually, she broke open previously unknown villages in the jungles because of her persistent leadership. She was a fully grown mature tree that produced shade, fruit, strong timber, and left a legacy for other growing leaders to follow.

It was Pauline's house that we moved into, her stove we cooked off, and her fledgling school that my parents took over to continue her work in. Where did she go? To another area in Liberia to develop a new life for others as well.

Visionary leadership is created by those who are unafraid to step into the dark.

Pauline is one of the touchstones now being used as a foundation of leadership for others to follow. Her footsteps are large and planted forever in the passing generations whom she still touches by her life.

Great power is a great thing, but a great human being is quite another.
— President Bill Clinton, speaking of Nelson Mandela

The coaches in your own life are training you in great leadership abilities for the future. How you handle the training determines the outcome. Don't quit, don't go backwards, and don't become discouraged, but see the big picture of your growing work and faith, allowing the training purposes to continue in your life.

There are many other lives you have not touched yet that will depend on your leadership skills in the future. Continue on…. Grow well. One day, others will stand on your shoulders and bless you for what you did for them.

QUESTIONS TO PONDER:

1. Who in your personal family has been a solid tree of leadership?

_____

_____

_____

_____

2. What have you learned from your family members' lives that has built your own?

_____

_____

_____

_____

3. Of those who have passed on, what has been their legacy to you?

_____

_____

_____

_____

4. And how do you plan to use their leadership in your own life?

_____

_____

_____

_____

13

Giving Up Is Not an Option

Smooth seas do not make skillful sailors.
— African Proverb

DETERMINATION

In the last chapter, I talked about how the building blocks of other leaders who have gone before us will create a solid foundation under us. If you are the first one to become a successful leader in your family, the legacy you leave behind will serve as the road map for them to follow you. When the leader within us starts growing upon an established underpinning, all sorts of paths open up to us.

Finding the right path comes as the inner nudges and desires are truly looked at and acknowledged. Most people ignore their dreams, thinking "*That* could never happen to me." Pushing away the small voice inside, they are unaware that *that* was the destiny they were designed to accomplish. Your dreams are the silent hints you have had your whole life about what and who you are to be. Listening and looking for those markers can become the beginning of the trek for significance in your life.

And when you know, that you know, that you know…nothing will be able to stop the determination within you. But the testing within certainly is a part of a leader's life. And being a leader means there will be many times you will need to reaffirm yourself to keep going, deciding that giving up is not an option.

Pauline Gruse discovered the land areas of the Kissi, the Kpelle, the Belle, and the Gbande tribes by her explorations. Her first trek was six weeks long with another single woman named Mildred; they went into the jungle with twenty people. Some were carriers and porters while others were youths and guides.

The jungles were alive with pygmy elephants, pygmy hippopotami, bush cats, and snakes, leopards, wild boars, and crocodiles. At times, she had to be borne on the carriers' shoulders through deep rivers because she would not turn back. She was afraid, but she pushed through her fears for the greater cause. After establishing Fassama as an outpost mission, she spent her days among the natives of the village, trying to understand and be understood.

Soon, she began to see that the witch doctors in the area were threatened by her presence. Trouble started happening to try to get her to leave. The government authorities had welcomed her because she could provide much needed educational skills and healthcare services. President Tubman of Liberia, who was an ordained Baptist minister himself, encouraged outpost missions to be established, knowing they would be the only chance to help his deeply impoverished nation to receive aid and education. This situation did not please the rural native rulers.

Pauline was met with opposition from these controlling factions because her message was one of freedom, education, medical care, and Christianity. The witch doctors could sense that her work would defeat their tyrannical hold over the people, and they would become the enemy over time. So they began a process to force her to leave... but nothing worked that they tried. She had no other options or places to go, so she stayed there through sickness, loss of helpers, loss of equipment, and lack of people. She stayed put.

One Monday morning, the drums began beating, and soon across the land, matching drums joined in. The atmosphere becomes heavy and oppressive when this happens, and the heaviness in the air makes it feel hard to breathe. The feeling of fear becomes tangible and people usually stay in their huts. The missionaries knew they were "playing a medicine." For seventy-two hours, the drums beat without stopping. At noon on Thursday, a strange cloud came over the mountain; the sky was clear and dry with only this black cloud drifting in. It became black with a greenish and yellow tinge to it. A booming and thundering began that became loud and deafening. The atmosphere became filled with fear. Ma Gruse, as they called her, was standing on her porch, giving instructions to some young men when a ball of lightning fell directly on her, knocking her to the ground.

Pauline tells of leaving her body and seeing the young men crying and falling on her body to pray. She heard beautiful music and the sound of choirs singing and a voice spoke to her as she ascended upwards. "Your work is not finished; you must go back." She did not want to return, but she did come back into her body, as alive as she had been before the lightning strike, which amazed the mission kids, her helpers, the villagers, the chief, and most of all, the witch doctors.

Her work continued on, and the people who created this attack against her finally concluded their efforts to force her out. Her enemies accepted the fact that "We have worked every medicine against the mission, but nothing can hurt the God people." In the end, respect was won, and with painstakingly small steps over time, the people began to accept the outside world as one of goodness and information that they could accept.

The main things are to suffer without becoming discouraged.
— François Fénelon

When quitting is not an option, a leader has to stay in command at all times.

If the superstitious fears of the people were to be replaced, one could not walk in fear before them. Once walking into a strange and unknown village, Pauline had the Chief of the village stride up to her and only stop abruptly when right in her face. His glaring eyes stared directly into hers, and with his breath full on her face, he grunted words in broken English between clenched teeth, demanding to know why she was there. She had to stand firm and not break eye contact, although she was trembling and her legs shaking so badly from fear of him. Keeping her tone of voice as gentle as possible, she told him she was just passing through and needed to spend the night. His eyes of fire suddenly softened and he gave her a hut for the night. His fear of her, and her fear of him ended quickly.

When there are no options to back down, a leader just has to keep going forward.

WHEN YOU CAN'T GO BACK

My family's first Christmas in the jungle was an unforgettable experience. It was to be a special day that our family would enjoy together. Dad stayed at the mission with us for the day, and we tried to relax as a family. Mom had decided that for our Christmas treat we would have popcorn and Kool-Aid. There was nothing to make presents out of and food was limited, but she had these two things somehow stashed away and brought them out, trying to cheer her family up.

The Africans had no idea what Christmas was; nor were they especially interested to know. But Mother invited them anyway, trying to make a special holiday for us and to share it with them. They didn't have birthdays or holidays of their own; every day was the same in their lives. The only time of celebration was when a hunter brought big game home because then everyone was excited to have fresh meat to eat. So it was going to be special the way she shared the birth of Christ with them through popcorn and cherry Kool-Aid.

We spent the steamy day homesick, wishing to see our families, and thinking of the joyful times they all were having back home. The lack of special food and no presents affected us children as we remembered Christmases previously experienced. We knew everyone who celebrated Christmas across the world was eating a huge plate of goodies and treats galore. It just made our hungry tummies growl more.

When the evening arrived, the natives slowly started coming to our house. Mom was thinking, "This is going to be good; they will love this!" As she popped the popcorn, the natives could hear the popping sounds; questioning frowns spread across their faces as they looked at each other in a quandary. Meanwhile, Mother made the red Kool-Aid and sweetened it with juice.

Then she brought it outside for all of us to have a special Christmas treat together. We kids started eating ours with great relish, enjoying one popcorn bite at a time and sipping our drinks with tiny little swallows to make the Kool-Aid last as long as possible.

When the Africans were given theirs, each one reluctantly accepted. They didn't try to eat the popcorn but talked among themselves, looking suspiciously at the white puffed corns and the red drink as if we were trying to poison them. We encouraged them to try it…

by eating in front of them. They had great discussions among themselves, looking at us and holding their "party" drinks and popcorn in their hands.

When we couldn't get them to go ahead, we just silently ate in front of them, watching to see what they would do. They were watching us and we were watching them. Mother's feelings were starting to be hurt because they were acting suspicious of us. They were talking urgently in a dialect to each other but not taking their eyes off us. Finally, one of them was brave enough to try his popcorn while the others watched him carefully. When nothing happened to him, the rest stood and gravely began to eat their popcorn. No expressions on their faces, no surprise, not even a "Wow, this is good!" No one said anything. They just politely ate it while staring at us.

Then the same thing happened with the red drink. There were more conversations among them, and more looking at us as if we were trying to trick them into something bad. Now that I think about it, maybe the red color made them think it was blood. We could tell they didn't want to try it, but they knew we were expecting them too. So they tasted it but made no expressions. With impassive faces, they slowly drank it down as if it were the worst possible thing they had ever had.

This Christmas celebration certainly did not have the effect we had thought it would. It was a very solemn and grave experience. No one spoke about liking the treats—no smiles…nothing. And when they finished eating our rare treat, they simply walked off into the dark with strange looks on their faces. No "Thank you for sharing with us." Nothing. Looking back, it must have been so awkward for my parents.

My mom was disappointed in the natives' response and felt like she had wasted our valued and only treat on them. It was yet another indication of how far apart our cultures really were. And it brought an even greater loneliness to her heart. Their silence and lack of response to her efforts made her feel rejected.

The villagers' inability to communicate with us and our inability to communicate with them caused a gap that night. We never did know if they liked the popcorn and Kool-Aid since no one ever said anything about it.

Our response to others can increase our chances to bond with them, or bring a greater distance between us.

Doubt not only rides in the vehicle of disappointing experiences, but it can get out and stand in front of a leader to try to stop his progression. I remember all of us trooping back into our hot house and mother's disappointment and regret for giving them our special treat. We went to bed in silence that Christmas night. There were no options to quit; we just had to keep going forward. But I'm sure the negative words of my grandparents about what would to "happen to you in Africa," were ringing in my parents' ears that night.

Little things have the power to break big dreams if we let them.

The next day, my parents continued their work with the same people who had shown us disrespect the night before. They acted as if nothing had occurred and treated the Africans as usual. They had an ironclad protection around their hearts that kept them focused, no matter what circumstances brought.

DOUBT DEFEATS DREAMS

Eventually, we moved to Monrovia, the capital city of Liberia, to provide a school and build a church where young adults could come out of the jungle to begin their futures. And we lived in an area that seemed to be the right place for children to be safely raised. But soon after moving there, a Pan American jet crashed close to our house, killing some fifty-three people, while forty-one survived. The four-engine DC8 jetliner went down in flames.... We as children were not allowed to leave the house while the survivors and the deceased were collected from the ground and trees around us.

The accident was a terrible shock to us after living in the jungle with only natives, animals, and birds around. My parents held warranted discussions about whether they had made the right decision to move from the jungle. "Were our children safer here? Did we bring them to the right area?" My parents had to live with the horror of what they were seeing right in front of our house.

Just as blinders are put around the eyes of a horse to keep him from getting distracted in a race, so a leader will at times have to put blinders on his own eyes to stay focused on his purpose.

Our house next to the airport had three bedrooms. I had my own room, which was closest to the front of the house and the farthest away from the family. My brothers all stayed in the same little bedroom down the hall. My parents had their bedroom at the very end of the hall. We were happy with the house because we didn't have to sleep under mosquito nets anymore, and we greatly appreciated having electricity at last.

One night while we were all asleep, a thief broke into our house and robbed us. This act was intended to stop us from accomplishing our goal, but my parents were leaders who refused yet again to back down. In Liberia, thieves commonly take all their clothing off and pour oil liberally all over their skin. If someone should catch them, it is impossible to hold onto them, so they are fairly certain they can escape easily.

The thief entered our house and went straight into my bedroom, naked and dripping in smelly oil. He came to my bedside, searching for anything of value. He emptied my special little box on the bed right next to my head. Oil dripped onto the sheets as he bent over, trying to see what he could take. The sleeping little golden-haired girl was right there at his mercy. He could have stolen me in the night, yet I was untouched and deeply asleep. I never felt his actions next to me. Only the oily sheets were proof of his presence that night.

He then crept down the hallway and entered my brothers' room, leaving trails of dirty oil along the floor. Finding nothing and leaving each little boy unharmed, he went to the door of our parents' room—finding it locked. He then went to the living room and proceeded to take everything he could find. Oily marks were all that remained of our precious few belongings. We lost our "missionary equipment" that night, the biggest losses being our microphones, guitar, amp, and most importantly, our food.

He took a lot of things except our precious lives—a special barrier existed between us and him, and he could not touch our precious lives. We seemed safer in the jungle than the city! We simply had to start over without our equipment and refuse to quit!

Opposition comes to all leaders; no matter who you are or where you go, it's to be accepted and expected.

DETERMINATION

One afternoon, Marvin, my middle brother, was riding Alan's bicycle along the roadside when suddenly a taxi swerved out of the road and hit him! He bounced up on the hood of the car, hit the windshield, flipped over the roof, and fell off behind the car. The impact knocked the wind out of him, but as soon as he could, he jumped back up. He was about eight years old at the time.

The taxi driver jumped out and rushed to him, furiously attacking him verbally for "hitting my taxi." Marvin was shocked that the man didn't check to see whether he was hurt, and in the adrenaline of the moment, my brother simply left the ruined bike there and took off running for home.

The enraged driver now jumped back into his taxi, with the dented hood, and tried to chase down my brother! Marvin was running as fast as he could, trying to look behind him at the pursuing car… terrified that the driver was going to hit him again. He did make it home, but just barely, before the taxi driver slammed on his brakes in the yard, jumping out after him.

Marvin ran into the house, screaming and crying in terror of the man. My dad jumped out of his chair and grabbed my brother to see whether he was okay. Marvin was bruised, but otherwise fine, except for the taxi driver who had really scared him and was now running up to the house to grab him. The taxi driver shoved open the house door, shouting that Marvin had hit his car and now he wanted to be paid for his damaged vehicle.

My dad tried reasoning with him, only to be met with belligerent cursing and yelling. This response instantly increased the stress level in the room for everyone. Marvin was crying hysterically. Mom was trying to figure out whether he was hurt. Dad was now raising his voice to be heard by the irate man who was yelling at the top of his lungs.

Suddenly, all patience fled the scene as my dad picked the man up by the seat of his pants, hauled him out of the house, and threw him out into the yard. Dad told the taxi driver in no uncertain terms, "If you don't leave this moment, I will have you thrown in jail for hitting my son." The man staggered to his feet, glaring and deciding that if he didn't want the police involved, it would be better to leave.

My parents were shocked, asking, "Since when did the rules change for driving so that the pedestrian now has become responsible for a car hitting him?" The rules hadn't changed, as we later discovered, but Africa was subject to changes day-by-day at times. Our little eyes took it all in.

Fear turns into courage; courage turns into determination, and determination turns into leadership in a matter of minutes.

These incidents only gave us greater resolve not to let the "bad guys" win and stop us from our assignment in life.

When the leader within you refuses to budge, things change.

As a leader, you will come to places in life where it would be easier to back down and quit. But then the purposes for which we started would be unfulfilled, and the many lives we are destined to touch would go untouched. If not you, then who? Set your mind in indomitable faith. Let your faith carry you when necessary. Know that your purpose will be accomplished. And never…never…never…never quit. You never know what tomorrow will bring. Seasons change; night does end, bringing fresh hopes, new surprises, and a brand new day to start again on your dreams.

Winners are those who decide they will never quit....

QUESTIONS TO PONDER:

1. If you know opposition will happen, how will you prepare to meet it?

_____

_____

_____

_____

2. If the greatest weapons could be used against you and still not stop your destiny, what would you do to promote your cause?

_____

_____

_____

_____

3. Finding strength comes from somewhere.... Where does yours come from?

_____

_____

_____

_____

14

Turning Desperation into Creativity

The lion does not turn around when a small dog barks.
— African Proverb

You already have what it takes to be a leader; you are born with a destiny and a desire to achieve that destiny. Your ability to chart the way ahead and then lead out is how leadership starts forming in your life as a child. The old African advice to leaders likens them to lions—the ones in charge of the jungle—and lions don't back down, nor even look at game too small to capture and eat.

A functioning leader has the option to quit many times, but it has been firmly decided in maturity that desperation will not end his purpose. Once the refusal to quit is achieved, new territory opens up. And once that occurs, subconsciously, creativity will always offer its help in solving the problem.

When there is no back door, creativity finds a way to solve an issue every time.

JUNGLE LEADERSHIP

Before their languages were in written form, there was no simple way to educate the tribes of native people. Speech was the only way to communicate. Each time something was to be taught, it had to be said over and over and repeated by the student over and over. The drive of leaders and their sheer force of will often warred against all forms of darkness and literally shoved the door open in West Africa for thousands to find the outside world. It was very difficult to combat the ignorance, village traditions, and superstitions that controlled the people with fear.

Leaders sacrificed, physically working from sun up to sundown seven days a week. My dad never took a day off—he felt his time was limited and should be spent building, preaching, singing, working, teaching, mentoring, correcting, showing, talking, praying, digging, laying rock, and sharing over and over for years and years.

Because we had a plane, the government had requested that we help the chiefs across Liberia by providing an air taxi service for them. A small fee was charged to pay for the fuel, and at times, it was the only form of support that sustained us since donations from home were not enough. But it meant that Dad was at the chiefs' beck and call whenever they wanted to go somewhere.

On one of these trips, Dad was landing the plane on a dirt landing strip to pick up another government official in a village called Belli Yella and fly him to Monrovia. While coming in for a landing and as the wheels touched the uneven ground, suddenly the right landing gear collapsed into a bugabug sinkhole. It had caved in when the landing gear touched the ground, and the instant hole had caused the landing gear to fall into this deep hole and snap. The gear folded up under the landing plane, and suddenly, the plane was tipping to the right and out of control, dragging the right wing on the ground. Pulling hard, Dad managed to get the plane to slow down and then stop. The little red and white Piper Tri-Pacer was down! The people came running to see what had happened. Talking, pointing, and edging closer, they watched my dad climb out of the plane, now tipped over with the right wing on the ground. Dad's heart was pounding, but the shock of it all didn't get a chance to kick in...because his adrenaline did!

CREATIVITY KICKS IN

Dad was bruised and scratched up a little but otherwise okay. With his mind racing as dark approached, he had to think on his feet. Remembering that he kept a small emergency kit onboard with a sharp machete, a shotgun, and ammo. Dad grabbed these items like they were made of gold! He took the machete to the bush nearby and cut down two trees, each about eight feet long. And using a volunteer from the crowd now gathered to watch what the white man would do, he lifted the plane's wing with his back, propped the plane's lowered wing up on a tree trunk, and put the other tree trunk under the other wing. Now the plane was sitting up again, and thank God, the wing hadn't suffered any damage. But the landing gear could not be bent back out—it was broken.

Looking at the crowd as his mind worked on how to get out of this jam, Dad saw a man sitting on an old worn-out bicycle with a little tool bag on its back. Dad walked over to the man and motioned to see the tool bag. It had an old worn-out wrench inside, a broken clawed hammer, and a pair of worn thin pliers. My dad used these to beat and bang the brake line loose and get the gear disconnected.

There was no radio contact there—the closest place with a radio was thirty-five miles away. There was no way out of there now except to walk! So Dad went to the chief in the village to ask for help to get to the Lutheran Mission thirty-five miles away. He offered to pay for a guide to help him get there. The chief sent him with a soldier with a machine gun who knew the way through the jungle footpath, and since there was a prison there, a prisoner who had a chain around his leg attached to a heavy log to carry the landing gear.

Dad and the soldier took the prisoner to a barber first to cut big patches of hair off his head. Big bare scalp circles would let everyone know he was a prisoner if he escaped. Before daylight the next morning, the chief put the log on one of the prisoner's shoulders and the broken landing gear on the other one and said, "Go!"

So they went through the jungle, the three of them in single file. Halfway through the day, they came to a village that offered them fish heads and a little rice. The three of them were fatigued, having lost so much fluid through sweating; their hands were swollen and heavy, and their feet and legs hurt from walking for miles. The prisoner was struggling to carry both heavy pieces while the leg iron was rubbing his leg raw. Dad's imagination had to be reined in as he worried what this man had done to deserve such punishment. He also worried about whether he would make it all the way to the mission. But his creativity had already gotten the landing gear off, and he had a guide and a carrier for the gear, so in desperation, he simply had to press on ahead.

WORRY DRAINS ENERGY

Dad struggled to continue walking as he dealt with heavy thoughts of concern for Mom, who was sick at that time and alone in Fassama with us four children. She did not know where he was. Without a way to let her know anything—even that he was alive—Dad could only keep marching. Watching the prisoner marching with a gun in his back, while being forced with every step to carry a heavy log on one shoulder and the precious landing gear on the other, Dad could have easily become discouraged and given up.

His worry was draining his energy. Would the plane still be intact when he got back, or would it have been stripped to bare metal by hungry Africans looking for anything of value? Walking through the contaminated streams and rivers and cutting down thick vines to blaze their path was a hard experience to go through. Whatever was in the water was getting into the cuts and scrapes he now had. Sweating through wet clothing chafes the body as well as works against one's energy. Many a desperate prayer went up through the jungle trees that day. It seemed like a nightmare that would never end.

At times, it's best not to think of what you can't change and just keep walking.

Lions don't turn around when the small dog barks! This amazing feat represented three miles an hour in austere circumstances for the three of them. In fourteen hours, from pre-dawn till late in the day, they managed to walk all thirty-five miles on a jungle footpath.

Exhausted, they staggered onto the Mission Compound of the Lutheran Church of Liberia as if they had made it to Heaven! There they found compassionate help, food, cool purified water to drink, clean clothing, a radio to call with, and beds to collapse in.

The leaders at the mission were helpful in getting Dad back in touch with his family, as well as finding the right tools for fixing the plane.

Upon his return, Dad found the plane still intact, just as he had left it. He fixed the landing gear by himself and flew home to us. He then got up the next day and flew the official where he needed to go. Back to work, a little stiff and sore, but made stronger by the experience, Dad had turned his desperation into creativity.

LEADERSHIP NEVER QUITS

It was hard, tough, mean, craggy, and rough work to open the interior of Africa in the '50s and '60s. And it took strong leadership that just would not give up, but doggedly worked to soften the hard hearts and open the eyes of those imprisoned by obscurity.

When desperation hits…genius creativity also shows up.

LEADERS LEAD THEMSELVES

Late one night when our daughter, Angela, was six weeks old, I was worrying about crib death happening to her. My husband was due to leave on a trip to the neighboring country of Zambia the next morning to smuggle food to a missionary family in desperate need. I knew they needed his help, so I didn't want to add pressure to make him feel bad about leaving me alone with a tiny baby. But I was worried. I didn't know that he also was worried about leaving me alone with our newborn.

During the night, my husband suddenly awoke to see a tall, blond man standing beside Angela's crib. The man spoke to my husband, telling him to go do his work while he would take care of the child and her mother. Afterwards, my husband realized this was an angel sent to protect us in the drama about to happen.

The next day when my husband told me about the experience, it lifted a huge weight off my shoulders. I was able to kiss him goodbye, confident that Angela would be just fine. He left that day with food fully packed in every crevice of the Land Rover. He picked up a buddy, and then the two of them drove through the bush, staying off the roads as they crossed over the border between Zimbabwe and Zambia. Bumping through the rough terrain, watching out for unusual signs of terroristic activities, they thought they had been unseen.

But before they got deeper into Zambia, while looking for a road to jump up on, the Zambian army caught and arrested them for spying. Suddenly, all of life changed. They were handcuffed and roughly handled and their vehicle seized. Taken to a nearby town, they were thrown in jail along with others who had been rounded up for various charges. The border was highly dangerous between these two nations because the war was coming to a close and the whites were suspected of wrongdoing in an effort to stop the process of handing over the government.

At twenty-seven years old and finding himself in a desperate situation, my husband had to trust and wait on how this situation would end. He thought, "At least I know my wife and child will be safe," as he remembered the dream he'd had the night before.

False accusations were thrown at him and the Land Rover was torn apart as the army looked for anything contraband. The food was scattered out and taken by some officials who also were hungry. Wanting every connection they could find, the army officials interrogated my husband and his friend with intense scrutiny. What was an American doing on the border of a country at war? The answer of feeding people was not good enough for them. Finding a handgun that had been stashed for protection, they seized on it as the only reason they could find to keep my husband and his friend in prison.

171

Their lives now at stake, again prayers of desperation were offered up. Being fed only raw peanuts and questionable water, my husband lived in undeniable fear for his life.

Back home, tiny Angela and I were recovering from childbirth, and I was wondering what was taking him so long to get back. He should have been back days ago. But knowing about the angel that had been seen over Angela's bed gave me complete trust that all was okay. I stayed in the house and never left; with the political chaos happening all around the city, it was far safer not to go anywhere. So I rationed out my food and just took care of our baby.

One morning, waking up in his nightmare, my husband noticed something green in the top pocket of his grimy and very dirty white shirt. Looking down in amazement, he saw it was a crisp $100 American bill. He did not have any money—it had all been confiscated when he was arrested. How did it get there and what could he do with it? It was the creative miracle needed in this worst hour of his life.

Out of his desperate situation came a creative idea. Talk the guard into accepting the money in exchange for the Land Rover's keys, opening the doors to both their cells, and looking the other way! Soon my husband had his chance when the guard came to interrogate him again. With a prayer in his heart, a bright smile on his face, and courage in his mind, my husband showed the guard his pocket and led the guard's mind to the creative solution—how this money could help him take care of some of his family's personal needs.

The guard greedily agreed to do it. Suddenly, the keys appeared, the doors opened, and my husband and his friend ran out of the darkened jail. Rushing to the vehicle and jamming the keys in with their hearts in their throats, they started the engine and backed out, trying not to attract attention. And as soon as they cleared the town, they got off the road and roared into the bush, racing toward Zimbabwe. The adrenaline! The fear! The scariness of it all! And now the release made these two wild to get back to safety!

They did make it safely back home. But it would be over ten years before my husband's intestinal health would return from the bacteria he endured in that horrific prison experience.

You may feel like you are walking through a maze of your own right now. Life looks dark and you are alone, but keep walking. *Leaders just keep walking and talking to themselves in their desperate hours.* Remind yourself that night cannot last forever; the dawn does come to all of us in time. Your developed faith will carry you through such times as these.

Talk to yourself. Look at your past and see how far you have come already on this footpath. Keep your eyes on the goal and refuse to look at the current circumstances. Just keep on walking...you have already taken off the landing gear called "Mistake," and you know the direction in which you need to go for help. Right now, the guide called Time is pushing you along at an uncomfortable pace, but movement is happening. And Creativity is beside you, helping you through the whole experience. Never fear...God is on your side. Your work in life and your faith will be strengthened by this experience when it is over. And your leadership skills will be honed to a new sharp edge for the future.

Growth happens when we refuse to quit.

Talk to yourself and look for creative solutions in your desperate hours. The old African proverb resonates that leaders are lions and problems are but small dogs yapping at us.

QUESTIONS TO PONDER:

1. How did you solve a past leadership experience using creativity?

_____

_____

_____

2. Do you see yourself in leadership as a lion or a small dog?

_____

_____

_____

3. Are you easily stopped when adversity hits?

_____

_____

_____

4. How do you manage to keep walking when circumstances are against you?

_____

_____

_____

5. What has been the lasting value of every set of desperate challenges you have faced?

_____

_____

_____

15

Giving Out of Your Need

Do not tell the man who is carrying you that he stinks.
— African Proverb

MAKING LIFE EASIER FOR OTHERS

When you wait to find the time to change a life, it will never happen. Life happens…and then you find the time. Leadership skills are needed in the absolute toughest times of life. You may have had such times already. As a leader seeing others go through hardships, your question becomes, "What can I do as a leader to help others find answers?" Remember all of your experiences have led you up to this point. You do have the leadership within to draw on to help others at crisis points in their lives. Meeting the most basic of human needs is important because it means helping humanity with compassionate care.

In the jungle, my family had an old, black, iron woodstove. It had been carried over the mountain on the back of a hired porter, under the direction of Pauline Gruse, at the peril of his life. There was no other way to have a stove except to have it hand-carried for days through the jungle-covered mountains. The Africans laughed at this "useless tool" because they would build a fire on the ground; having done so for centuries, they could see no reason to change. But Pauline's foresight made my mother's life a little easier. We had to get the heat just right to cook on the stove without burning anything. That old fashioned stove did its best to ruin food every day, but at least we had one. Cooking was a challenge to say the least!

When we left the jungle and moved to Monrovia, my mother had no stove at all to cook on. With a hungry husband and four "starving" kids, all her time was spent constantly trying to keep us all fed. All she had was an old popcorn cooker and somebody's old worn-out electric skillet that had been shipped to us. That's it. She had to figure out how to cook every meal for six people with these two small appliances.

How many different meals did we have? We had a processed canned meat called Spam. We had Spam fried...Spam scrambled...Spam cooked in the skillet stewed with tomatoes, Spam cooked in the popcorn popper...Spam patties in the skillet with onions.... Eventually, Mom did get a stove. But she managed to keep us all fed with her popcorn popper and her electric skillet until that happened.

Never ignore the needs of those working to help people in Third World countries—you never know what they are really dealing with. Leaders don't complain; they hold their heads up and stubbornly find a way to keep going. Many times, they live on fast hope and a prayer in the unfolding drama of the moment. Their needs are often only known by God. As a leader, my mother did not find it easy to live in Africa, yet she worked consistently to make life easier for us. Never think leaders don't need anything—they always do, and your help could make a difference to them.

PEOPLE ARE FRAGILE

Having people skills in a crisis is important because people are fragile and easily broken when their lives are shattered. While working in Haiti after the massive earthquake of 2010, I was caring for people in makeshift camps containing thousands of displaced people. These people had become so afraid of going inside buildings that over 1.5 million people were living outside. Having been through a strong aftershock in the middle of the night there myself, I couldn't blame them…. It was a fearful time to say the least for everyone in Haiti.

I had asked America to give me one million baby wipes to use in Haiti, and generous companies had given me two million. These were desperately needed by everyone because there was no water, or way to help cleanse wounds or provide a way to survive outdoors for a long amount of time. So I was walking through the camps, handing out containers of wipes and instant food packages to every mom with a young child. My shoulders were aching from lugging heavy shoulder bags of goods. The teams of volunteers were doing their best in different areas of Port Au Prince to help the people. My team was doing its best to keep up with all the people coming at me and the paths we were trying to thread through among the plastic sheeting and narrow aisles that the people had made themselves. It was becoming more difficult to move quickly through the crowd; the crush of people was growing fast, and I felt the need to move away from them.

So I decided to turn left and go around a corner to the next line of little "tents," looking for mothers with infants. There I saw the derelict back of a truck, just the box part, all torn up and left as damaged beyond repair. My eyes caught those of a desperate mother who had just given birth to a baby in that dirty, filthy truck bed. It shocked me and broke my heart instantly. I could not speak in French to her, nor she in English to me, but her heart and mine met in her worst hour of need.

Only another woman could have related to what was happening to her at that hour. I reached over to grab the one real towel I had in my supplies, and I wrapped the baby up and held the child, trying to comfort the mother. I just grabbed something to help her as quickly as I could. Then I saw another baby, about eighteen months old, sit up on the mother's other side and watch me with huge eyes. He was so dirty from the truck, and his mama was too. All she had was what I had brought her…. What if I hadn't come right then in her hour of need? What if I had chosen another little trail to follow instead of the one where a laboring woman was in the worst condition of her life? No one had directed me to her; I guess no one knew what was happening in all the chaos. But God knew one woman in the depths of need…needed me. I tried to be as tender as I could to her.

Reaching back in my mind to a faraway place in the deep jungles of Africa, I again saw Else Lund's hand tenderly touching suffering people. I felt the link of compassion hook my heart to those in my past, telling me again to help the helpless.

Giving as a leader can be the seed that gets planted in another generation, for another time and place to germinate and grow a tree.

BEING WHERE YOU ARE NEEDED

I will never forget that mother, nor the weight of a little newborn baby in my arms. I hated to leave her there in that truck bed. But there was nowhere to send her, so I loaded her with supplies and begged my helpers to please go back and check on her. Later, I found out her husband had been killed in the earthquake, and she and her little boy had found this truck bed and crawled up into it when her labor started. Looking at the truck before I left, I saw she would be dry and safe there, and maybe it was the best place for her to stay, even though it was so dirty and out of place for a newborn and an exhausted mother.

STAYING STEADY

This mother needed my loving support…and I just needed her to know I loved her. I still pray for her when I think of her and the experience we had together when her baby was born.

Using leadership skills when everything is in chaos is important to help people feel steadied and comforted, even if there are very little actual supplies to give them. You can still use your heart to comfort them.

Else Lund taught me that I still have my heart to soothe the brokenhearted and the suffering child. I can use my heart when there is nothing else.

DESTINY DNA

When I lost my second child due to a miscarriage, I was in the hospital for five days. I went through such grief over that child. And when I recovered enough to go back to "life," it was as if no one remembered I had been almost twenty weeks pregnant. I was back in my regular clothes and looked the same as before, but inside, the loss of that baby really hurt me. It was a private pain I could not share with others; nor did anyone talk with me about the loss. The ignoring of our baby's death made it that much more painful to endure alone.

Finally, after months of this deep grieving, I was again crying for my baby the week when the baby should have been born. Then I heard a quiet, small voice say to me, "If you give up your desire to have another baby, I will give you children all over the world."

I suddenly stopped crying when I heard this amazing statement. And I thought about it for a while…and then I made a deal with God: "Okay, I will stop grieving and put him in your hands if you make this possible for me." I was able after that amazing conversation to let my child go and move on. *I gave my baby out of my need that day to God.* Over time, I gradually forgot about the conversation completely.

Some twenty-five years later, I was driving to our warehouse to check on another load of food being shipped out to needy children in another country. I was sitting in silence at a red light when I heard that same sweet little voice say to me, "Remember my promise to give you children all over the world?"

In amazement, I suddenly realized that Moms Against Hunger, which I had founded, had been feeding children, and I had been holding babies and caring for them in so many different nations…the promise had come true! The leader within me shed some tears that day as it all came back to me, and I saw the completion of my destiny to care for humanity. Moms Against Hunger was my destiny…. From the DNA of my earliest days, my life had been destined to do this work.

WHEN FOCUS BECOMES CLEAR

As a young girl, Anne Frank did not know she would leave a mark worldwide with her small diary. *She gave, out of her need, her thoughts on paper.* She could not foresee that her private little thoughts were not really for her; they were for all of us around the world. She left a lasting legacy in her short lifetime—the opportunity for us all to see the incredible circumstances that unfolded for children during Hitler's reign of terror. She wrote the following eight words to encourage the wealthy nations of the world to stand up to tyranny for the helpless:

No one has ever become poor by giving.
— Anne Frank

Everyone has a place to fulfill, a hardship to endure, a life to live. Yours and mine as leaders requires us to do more than just watch. We cannot just "be".... We must "do" to offer solutions, to bring about change, to lessen the darkness and brighten the eyes of the downcast.

Growing the leader within you is achieved by developing into the greatest person you can be, with life's entire myriad of experiences giving you a wealth of knowledge to draw from to serve the world around you.

In the hearts of mature leaders will be the desire to give, out of their past needs they have lived through, and for the betterment of others in need.

QUESTIONS TO PONDER:

1. Have you ever had to go without a need being met for an extended time?

_____

_____

_____

_____

2. Is this need something you have seen a child also go through?

_____

_____

_____

3. If so, what power do you have to change that child's life right now?

_____

_____

_____

4. If leadership is the way needs can be met, how can your leadership effect change in this area in the future?

_____

_____

_____

5. To be a leader means to be where you are needed. Where are you needed?

_____

_____

_____

6. What would be the greatest way you could impact the world?

_____

_____

_____

7. What is your Destiny DNA?

_____

_____

_____

8. Have you ever had an epiphany moment? If so, what was it?

_____

_____

_____

16

Dreaming with Eyes Wide Open

*All men dream, but not equally. Those who dream by night in the dusty
recesses of their minds, wake in the day to find that it was vanity:
but the dreamers of the day are dangerous men, for they may act on
their dreams with open eyes, to make them possible.*
— T. E. Lawrence

Leadership brings you to pivotal points when your heart will feel
constrained to do something for the earth's needs. Like a child's dot-
to-dot game where a line has to be drawn between numbered dots to
reveal the hidden picture, so our lives as leaders also reveal a picture
in time. When connecting the dots in your mind, the seeds, which
have lain dormant in your life, begin to germinate and show green
life. You will then know how you are designed to help the world
around you.

UNFORGETTABLE SIGHTS

As a child living in Africa, I saw small children just like me, except
their naked bellies were swollen and they suffered from many diseases. I could see the difference in how they looked, even though we

were close in age and height. They were little girls and boys with spindly legs, skinny arms, and giant tummies. We played together while they often had terrible coughs and running sores on their bodies. I remember how we fought against the flies that followed us while we tried to play together as children. Holding hands and running together, I remember the little girls' hands were rough, very dry, and often dirty, yet we were all kids and tried to understand each other despite language problems and vastly different cultures. It seemed everyone was always hungry, even us.

> *Pretend you are dead and you will see who really loves you.*
> — African proverb

Let me ask you a question: Does it hurt your heart when you see a child crying and in pain? Can you walk past a handicapped person without feeling a twinge that you really should do something for him or her? Are you able to empathize with those who have lost their possessions or their health in a tough situation?

Things that make you weep can be the sign of a nudge to help solve an issue in the world.

I SEE A NEED FOR ADVOCACY

Getting an emergency phone call late one night when I lived in Illinois, I rushed to the hospital to find a horror-stricken child who clung to me in terror. A neighbor told me the story that I could hardly take in. This little eight-year-old girl was a child from one of my weekly classes for children. Her mother was a prostitute who tried to keep her two daughters alongside her during her rough life. I believe this mother loved her children, but she had no real support from outside people to help her make good decisions. The children's class, which this little girl and her sister attended, seemed to be the only

186

sane thing in their lives, and both of them had bonded with me as their leader. Their mother allowed them to come, seeing how much they enjoyed the class.

The mother had moved into a rented apartment with a man who turned out to be deranged. He had hated the girls immediately, and over a short period of time, he made their lives miserable. One night, the man and woman had an argument in the bedroom, and he began beating her and throwing things. Then he lost all control and beat her to death.

The children heard what was happening and ran to the door, crying and banging on the door for him to open it. Throwing open the bedroom door, he rushed at the girls, shouting at them. He had a knife, which he quickly used to stab the older girl, slashing her throat and killing her in front of her little sister.

Terrified, the younger sister ran for her life, not knowing, as an eight-year-old, what to do to protect herself; instead of running outside for help, she ran upstairs and hid in the farthest corner she could find in a dark closet. The man began to go from room to room, searching for her and screaming that he would find her and kill her too. She could hear him downstairs, but she thought she was safe, squeezed as far back as possible in the closet's corner. She kept wishing for Mommy to come and save her, not knowing yet that her mother lay dead in the downstairs bedroom. Fortunately, the loud commotion had woken the neighbor, who was too afraid to come over, but had called the police for help.

The searching man couldn't find the little girl, which enraged him more, so while the police were en route to get there, he began to stomp his way up the stairs, yelling and cursing and telling the little girl that he would find her no matter where she was.

This child could hear him coming and began crying in sheer fright. When he heard her, he came to the closet and opened the door. Then he grabbed her, pulling her out of the closet. He began slashing at her with the butcher knife all over her body. She was screaming and kicking and trying to get away from him while he had a death grip on her. When the police arrived and stormed the apartment, she was still screaming, and his shouts for her to "hold still" could be heard below.

The man was quickly subdued by the police, and the hysterical child, covered in blood, lay trembling on the floor with her eyes wide open. She was rushed to the hospital where I was called to come because I was the only one she kept calling for. My name was all she could say, over and over.

I walked in and saw her covered in bandages, with silent tears pouring down her face while she lay there in the clean white sheets, making a little groaning sound and trembling. She saw me and reached her little arms up to me, with the worst look on her face that I have ever seen on a child. I held her as best I could so I would not hurt her wounds. I didn't have any words to say, so I just cried and cried with her. No human being should have to go through something like this, much less a child. Each day, I went to the hospital to comfort her and try to ease the horror she had been through. I remember thinking, "Am I dreaming? Is this really happening?"

In the week that followed, my husband performed the saddest two funerals. I was at a loss how to comfort the little girl whose life had been shattered by adults. That nightmare put a desire in me yet again to do something for suffering children who are so vulnerable to the actions of the adults around them.

I see a need for warmhearted, caring individuals who are passionate about helping the helpless to be involved in humanitarian work.

People who do not view their work in human services as a cold 9 to 5 job. Too many children have fallen through the cracks of systems because no one with a heart was really involved in caring for them. Children are not a paycheck, but real, living, soft little lives that will harden into the shapes that adults have formed them into.

I SEE THE NEED FOR FOOD

Just the smell of raw rice takes me back to memories of my African childhood. No such thing as a store existed since we lived sixty-five miles from any road! So I remember watching the process of rice being cut and thrashed from heavy green heads to remove the rice.

Come with me to the jungle and let me show you how a mother feeds her children there. She works for hours each day—it's very strenuous…it's hot and steamy…sweat runs down into your eyes, down your hairline, and down your back, non-stop. Flies and mosquitoes are constantly trying to land and bite and sting. The air smells of unwashed bodies…and wet mud and moldy plants in the hot sweltering sun. Often, the children have swollen bellies and feel the deep pain of unending hunger. We walk into the field and watch for deadly snakes and rodents to attack…the cassava snake or the mamba snake is deadly, and if we accidently are bitten…death will happen in minutes. Pull off the heads of grain that are still on the plant even if they are half-eaten by water rats, or the leftovers from locusts or wild bees. The need to find food is a race against mildew, insects, rodents, birds, and animals, all of which are looking for food all day… every day. With her bare hands (no tools) and often with a baby on her back, I have watched African mothers struggle for survival, and sometimes, lose.

The mother gathers the meager amount of grain…if enough can be found for a meal…and takes it back to her hut to grind with a mortar and pestle. It is "chopped" in big, tall wooden hand-carved containers. When the rice is clean of its outer husk, it is fanned up in the air to rid it of all lingering pieces of husk and any bugs. I would hear the women and girls beating the rice hulls with alternating thrusts of their long poles into the wooden containers; sometimes, two would be working in one large wooden base made of solid tree trunks; these wooden bases were very important to each family's kitchen. Thunk, thunk. They would beat and sing a song to the rhythm of their work. This was backbreaking work since they would beat up and down for sometimes long periods of time. It could take up to thirty minutes of pounding and pounding to break the husk from the single grains of rice. The weighty wood thumping the bottom of the wooden container makes a heavy sound. The mother is soaked with sweat from pounding it out, and her stomach clenches in pain…. Finally, the precious rice in the bottom is carefully scooped out with her hands and put in a homemade, oblong, shallow reed basket.

I can hear the swishing sound of the older girls expertly throwing the rice up and down, up and down, to fan it thoroughly so no bugs are cooked with the rice. The wind blows away small particles, while other rice falls from the basket's edges into a cardboard box to be resifted again so no precious food is lost. Every grain is of value. Slapping mats of rice up in the air, trying to catch the wind to blow out the thousands of bugs and the broken husks intermingled with the pounded rice, these mothers carry out this dance for food. I have watched mothers in Third World countries do this over and over. It's the *only source* of food…and for most, the *only type* of food they will have for seasons at a time. Often, the chief will have to be given his part before they can take theirs for their children.

Fanning our food was an everyday event because the bugs frequently and aggressively invaded our supplies. No one ever refused to do rice fanning; we all knew its value.

The struggle to survive is great, and the painful growling abdomens of human beings enforces the ability to eat anything at times. Bug wings and bodies are often left in the rice because the mother can't get them all out…or she simply does not have the energy to keep tossing the rice in the air. And when it's cooked over the fire…sadly, it's just rice…carbohydrates and nothing more. No protein, no vitamins, no amino acids, no minerals…simply rice. And unless the men can catch the wily monkeys or the rare animal once in awhile, the rice is all they will have to eat. It will fill a child's tummy for another day, but slowly, malnutrition and then starvation occur in the growing bodies of children who eat like this.

The women never minded the little white girl watching them work. They would look at me, smile, and never lose their rhythm. I wanted to help so they would hand me their worn wooden poles, warm and sweaty from their hands, to chop with. But I couldn't lift the heavy poles over and over several times. They would laugh at me and take back over again.

Still today in parts of Africa, the women are doing this same work. The average person never thinks of the natural work that goes into getting rice from the fields to the table. What a blessing to be able just to buy a bag at a store, take it home to my air-conditioned clean kitchen, open the bag, and simply pour some into a nice pan on my awesome stove and cook it!

All over the world, mothers must daily be vigilant, diligent, and hard, hard workers to feed their families. Seeing their many needs as a child would mark me for life with the desire to do something for hungry people.

In just one month of malnutrition and hunger, a young child will start sliding downhill physically. And then sickness reveals its ugly hand in her body, and her mind will only focus on one thing—finding something to eat. And if she doesn't get fed nutritious food, the body begins breaking down all muscles, trying to stay alive. The child's bones will become fragile, and her ability to walk will be painful as her body feeds on itself. Her hair will become patchy and could lighten, her arms and legs become spindly while her abdomen slowly swells. Then the pain begins, and she becomes weak and often catches viral or bacterial infections.

Every six seconds, a child dies from hunger-related illnesses.

Once in awhile, a family would have a special treat—monkey! The process back in the bush was to spear the monkey or shoot him with a shotgun. While monkeys were plentiful in every tree, they were also very wild and hard to catch. Once the animal did fall to the ground, the hunter would make a long slicing cut in the monkey's tail with a machete. Then he would take the tail and push the cut area over the head, creating a way to carry the animal easily like a knapsack, or a hairy purse.

Once back home, the hunter would throw the monkey on the rattan screen, which always hung over the fire. When I say "throw the monkey," I am talking about the whole animal—hair, head, entrails, hands, and feet—all of him! This monkey would smoke and smoke until slowly the hair would burn away (a terrible smell) and it would "cook." Our noses told us when a monkey had been on a fire for about three days. Not only was the look of it very distasteful, but the threat of it being spoiled and rotten (after three days in the sweltering humid heat), lent a smell that would take your breath away if the wind was just right!

The family would eat this meat for a day or so. How did they keep from getting sick? They didn't! There were lots of stomach problems, and dysentery was a part of life; they did not know that their diet was a big part of their problem. There was always sickness in the village, which was blamed on evil juju or sorcery happening against them, or possibly someone was poisoning them, which really was a possibility, or some other reason, but they never understood it could be caused by the food they were ingesting.

I SEE THE NEED FOR CLOTHING

The only way to get clothes dry in the rainy season was to hang them up under the roof where the pouring rain couldn't touch them. It takes a long time to dry clothing hanging outside in very humid torrents of rain. It could become moldy before it became dry.

The rainy season is violent and sheets of water pour down for days at a time. No one can work in it, so the natives stay inside their huts around steamy humid fires. Although we know that Pauline Gruse walked for days many times in the pouring rain without an umbrella to get to Fassama. One couldn't have held onto an umbrella if it had been available because of the deep mud and sliding and slipping along the path. But she would go anyway, soaking wet with the rain pouring down on her and her team, to teach in the faraway village of Fassama. Her determination to bring them aid was unstoppable. But for the people of the villages, the rainy season meant there was nothing to do but wait. Thus food stocks would become lower and lower as the season continued.

Once, my oldest brother Alan contracted one of the strange ailments that happens in Africa—painful worms in his knee. It happened because his pants had not been thoroughly ironed after being dried outside. Flying bugs had laid eggs in the jean fabric and burrowed into his skin when he wore the pants. Within days, sores had formed and a maggot was eating his flesh!

Like so many areas of need in the villages, the native manner of dress was something we had to get used to. While those who lived within the mission grounds had been clothed and fed daily, those who did not only wore what rags could be found. The men would wear the traditional loincloth and the women would have a *lapa lapa*, which was nothing but a length of cloth wrapped around the waist. It was common for children to be completely naked since they had nothing at all.

Granted, the climate was stifling, but the lack of clothing meant their skin was unprotected from the penetrating and damaging sunrays and no barrier existed between their skin and the enormous insect infestation. This lack of clothing helped to cause many sicknesses and diseases.

There was a huge need for clothing…. These people wanted clothes, but they often had no idea how or where to wear them. Once, we received a box of clothing, which we promptly gave out. A dress with long sleeves went to a lady in the village, who wore it to church the very next time. She was not told how to wear this garment, so she wrapped the sleeves around her waist and the dress trailed on the ground behind her.

Another and surprising "gift" shipped to us was an orange one-piece long underwear garment big enough to fit a man; a dangling flap in the garment's back had been held up by three buttons, but now only one button remained. Somehow, this garment was given to a native man, who wore it proudly. Often Americans had no concept of what actually would be useful. More than once I saw a woman wearing only a bra, proudly thinking she was dressed.

Stern paternal looks often came our way as children because we giggled over the outrageous things we saw. We didn't want to hurt the people's feelings, so we couldn't say anything, and we didn't have better clothing for them anyway.

I SEE THE NEED FOR CLEAN WATER

Certain types of vines produced water; when the vine was cut at an angle, water would run out and provide clean water pure enough to drink. Wise Africans taught Westerners many things about living in the jungle safely, such as how to find water in this way.

Someone once said, "It depends on what part of the world you are standing on as to how smart you are!" For example, if you took the city dweller and placed him in the jungle, he would not be able to survive. And if you took the African and placed him in the city, he would not know how to survive. But each in his own element could certainly help the other to gather new skills and survive the rigors of each life.

While setting up camp late in the day in South Africa, my husband and I were both tying down our little travel trailer as the shadows grew longer and longer. Trying to hurry so we would not be outside in a strange place after dark, we both worked feverishly. Suddenly, an odd thing happened. A little white boy with very white blond hair came up to me out of nowhere. He said to me, "Do you have a glass of water I can have?"

Sadly, I didn't have anything that I could stop and give him at the moment. We had no electricity yet because I was busy helping to set it up. When I turned to try to explain that if he gave me a little while, I would find him some, he had already disappeared into the dusk. I couldn't find him and never saw him again. Strange to see him in the middle of nowhere…and strange for him just as quickly to disappear.

I wonder whether his request was meant to make me conscious of thirsty people who needed water, compassion, training, and leadership? I have never forgotten him, and I can see his little face now. I have wished many times that I had stopped everything I was doing to give him water right then.

Having lived in several African countries, I have learned to watch carefully any health issues that occur. Waterborne infections, sick people, and environment issues must be taken seriously while living in the tropical heat.

I am very concerned about what is happening in Haiti and many areas of the world right now as I write this; please know that Moms Against Hunger has shipped enormous amounts of clean water and now is working on water purification systems. Digging wells is good, but when the water source is contaminated, greater danger exists for the innocent. Purified water is essential for life.

I SEE THE NEED FOR MEDICAL CARE

One of the serious issues in other countries is cholera. Spending time with a medical doctor while on a trip to Haiti, I learned that his greatest battle was with this terribly infectious disease. It affects a person with severe dehydration that will result in death due to the intense loss of all bodily fluids at the same time. Without immediate medical attention, it can result in death within hours after the symptoms begin. Cholera is a violent, contagious disease spread through contaminated food and water and through human contact. But it is easily treated with fluids and glucose, if antibiotics are not available. Cholera is suspected to be a plague, and it continues in poor countries today. Poverty, the lack of resources and hygiene, and poor sanitary sewage systems all play a role in this horrific disease. Precautions are essential, such as boiling water before drinking it or washing in it. Being careful of what is eaten and proper hand-washing are imperative for preventive protection.

Much education is still needed to teach the peoples of the world how to prevent various life-threatening challenges that plague their nations.

I SEE THE NEED FOR FARMING HELP

The hot sun burns through the dusky horizon and illuminates a tall thin mother already outside looking in a dried field for something... anything...a small morsel of corn...a bite of a locust...a leaf even. A hungry crying child can be heard in the morning dawn from where it lies under a rugged tree with leafless branches. The mother scratches the hardened ground with her stick and glances back at her son. He's still alive if he can cry.

Slowly, tears gather in her eyes; she blinks them back, trying to see the earth beneath her feet. "There must be something here the animals didn't get, or the others." The liquid pain overwhelms her ability to hold back the tears that come sliding down her gaunt face yet again—on yet another day in the fight against starvation.

The sun blazes as its full brunt now hits the earth and the heat forces the mother to walk to her son and hold him while she rests, needing her strength to pick up his small body. She cannot imagine there are leaders around the world who care and really do want to help her.

But those leaders just don't know how yet.... I hope to change that with this book in your hands. I'm dreaming with my eyes wide open....

Sitting outside with only mats covering the ground in a small village, native mothers and I have shared smiles, and the pure joy of being together again. What is so great about sitting with them in seemingly abject poverty? These women, while suffering greatly, have learned to cherish the smallest joys in life; they have a freedom from modern pressures, stresses, and anxieties, and they share each other's lives. Those living on the other side of the world for the most part do not experience this richness daily. Those women were happy just because I was with them on that afternoon. Seeing the pain in their eyes and their spirit, regardless, makes a leader willing to reach out to help. And a determined mother will do anything it takes to ease a child's pain.

QUESTIONS TO PONDER:

1. As a leader, how can you impact change in the world you see around you?

_____

_____

_____

2. What will be your platform to work on?

_____

_____

_____

3. Whom can you influence to help you in your cause?

_____

_____

_____

4. What single person is your target and contact to help?

_____

_____

_____

5. When is your target date for actually performing this act of compassion?

_____

_____

_____

17

Developing Courage Under Fire

There is no passion to be found playing small—in settling for a life that is less than the one you are capable of living.
— Nelson Mandela

PROPER UNDERSTANDING

Your strength and courage in leadership must be tempered with wise assessments of different situations. To try to step in and control an uncomfortable state of affairs cannot be done wisely without all the knowledge you need available. Usually, in expressing our opinions, we don't have all the facts. Before great swelling words pop out of our mouths, we need to know those facts. How to find proper understanding is something growing leaders must learn.

Good and bad things happen in life. The difference lies in how leadership takes the lead to control these things. The actions of both good and bad leadership leave repercussions, and if the reactions were negative, they must be turned into positives.

After the Rhodesian War, my husband and I often took visiting guests on sightseeing trips in Zimbabwe. We wanted to share with them our adventures and experiences. Some visitors were interested in our work while others came with their own agendas, often unable to see we were two worn-out young leaders who needed attention ourselves. We took some visitors to see the church project that my husband had been building right through the war. We were proud of it and the many risks that had gone into building this church, which could seat over four hundred people. Our visitors' lack of interest and constant pointing out of its defects didn't help two kids who needed encouragement. So we eventually quit showing our projects and just focused on what our visitors came to do.

One day while standing on the border between Mozambique and Zimbabwe, we were pointing out different places we had been and the things that had happened to us. Signs were posted clearly in English that photography was not allowed. Regardless, our guests brought out their cameras and started taking pictures. We tried to say gently, "Don't take pictures here." But they were oblivious to our advice and continued on. Angela was still a baby in my arms, so I couldn't do much but keep a squirming baby quiet.

Our guests were talking and laughing and did not seem to understand that they were putting us in danger. Then with sinking hearts, the two of us saw the border guards, with their guns pointed, marching toward us at a pace that meant business. They came up to us and straightaway demanded to know why "we" were taking pictures and breaking the law. "We" hadn't been—our guests had, but, of course, our guests now looked at us to get us all out of trouble.

The guests began to speak up and state their opinions of how innocent their pictures were. I held my breath, knowing the situation was escalating because the guards would see their arguments as resistance to their orders. Then, without a word, they seized both my husband and our male guest, and marched them away, leaving me, our baby, and our guest's wife to stand watching. The guards took the men at gunpoint into a building without windows.

I didn't know what was going to happen to them. Life was still very much at only a surface calm with white people not really appreciated nor wanted in the country. Too much bloodshed had happened, and the war was still a deep, fresh wound for everyone. Suspicion was everywhere and no one trusted anyone.

Our guest's wife was chattering, "I can't believe this…. We didn't do anything…. It's just a picture…. When are they coming back?" She did not realize that when you live in a foreign country, you are not in charge. In America, citizens enjoy many rights and freedoms, but it is not so in many other nations across the world. I tried not to add my nerves to the situation by giving her more reasons to be concerned. But I was concerned. Yes, they had disobeyed "just a simple sign" in their own eyes, but we had actually put them in harm's way by not explaining clearly enough or getting their agreement first to abide by all of this new country's rules. And now we were all in trouble for their rash choices.

Several hours passed as the guest's wife and I tried to keep our minds off what might be happening to the men. She wanted to go inside the building and find them, but I told her we couldn't do such a thing and must wait quietly outside. *Patience in a leader's life is a priceless jewel.* I knew we could be arrested too if we tried to intercede.

Finally, she dozed off in the car when the baby did…leaving me quietly in relief. The shadows grew long outside the car before we finally saw any motion. With great relief, the two men came outside, a bit shaken up but alive. Their interrogation was over, and thankfully, they had been released to us. I couldn't wait to get out of there. They had lost their cameras but not their lives. *Courage under fire means to keep steady when the pressure is on.*

Living in a heavily wooded area, I had brought some trash outside to burn. The trees were dry, and I had paid no attention to exactly how careful one must be to burn under those conditions. So I lit the fire in the barrel, put in the trash, and walked away. Soon an explosion happened, caused by a hairspray can in the fire. Flames leapt up and caught on fire the bark of a nearby tree. The flames raced up that tree in seconds and caught a second tree on fire. In a matter of minutes, I had a roaring fire jumping from tree to tree. I was truly scared and ran into the house to grab my daughter (we were home alone at the time). I made her go outside and sit at a safe distance while I started battling the blaze.

My efforts were to no avail. The fire got bigger and bigger. Suddenly, I realized our home was in danger, and so were we! My attempt to deal with the forces of fire and dry conditions by myself was putting our lives in jeopardy. Many volunteers ended up having to come out to cut a fire path around our land to guard the neighboring land and trees. It took most of the day to get the blaze out. I was horrified by what I had caused, and I became fearful of the power of fire. The seriousness of the situation forever "burned" in my mind the great care that must be taken or years of work can be lost due to negligence. *Courage under fire means utilizing the strength of others to help guide you in a crisis.* My leadership skills had made me try to solve the crisis by myself, which was the wrong decision to make.

At that time, I couldn't have known that in our future would be thousands of families who would lose everything but their lives to raging fires, and we would be able to help them through the shock of their experiences.

NUDGES

These nudges in understanding were packing into us the knowledge of how to help someone in need. It can be easy to miss the signs if the focus becomes inward and the thinking pattern stunted into self-protecting behaviors. It's when we look outside of our own experiences that we can see the markings of a preplanned destiny that started way back on the day we were born!

Courage under fire can mean making a right decision for the protection of others in danger.

During the civil war in Rhodesia, there was an extreme shortage of fuel and few people had cars since most relied on the city bus systems. The cost of gas—or petrol as it is called in Africa—was sky high, and those who were blessed enough to own vehicles rationed out their fuel carefully for necessary trips only. My family's funds were used to buy buses and provide transportation so people could get to us for training.

Regan, my youngest brother, had to develop courage under fire and tells this story:

> I was eighteen years old at the time, and it was my responsibility to drive the church bus in Salisbury, Rhodesia in Southern Africa. One night after church services, I was dropping off young people in a rough part of town. As I was about to stop for a drop off, I could hear the kids start yelling not to stop, and I saw about fifty men coming toward the bus from the shadows. So, I kept going, but the road was a dead end. So, I drove to the end of the road, which was about 400 yards from the men. The bus door was on the back of the bus. I stopped and told the kids who were supposed to be dropped off there to get out and run! The back door locked with a key, so I locked it.

It felt like it was taking me forever! Everything was in slow motion! I could see all those guys with machetes and bricks sprinting toward us. The kids got out, scattered like ants, and disappeared into the neighborhood.

I locked the door, got back into the cab, and shifted into first. I was just shifting into second when they caught up with us. They spread out across the road in order to stop the bus. Instead of stopping, I did my best to run them over! They scattered and got out of the way, meanwhile launching their bricks, and whacking the windows with their machetes, but I got us out of there unharmed.

This mob attack had started when on a previous bus run, one of the young men had kicked one of the girls in the face. So, I had made him ride in the front with me, separating him from the girl. I thought the incident was over. Well, it wasn't. She had gathered a huge gang of friends to capture and kill him that night. We barely escaped. Some of the kids on the bus recognized some of the gang members. So, when I got back to our mission church, I started working the phones. I called the police. I called parents. I called so many people!

Then within hours, the kids sent a message to the church: "The police are after us, and since no one was hurt, please would you not prosecute us?" The matter ended, and the young man turned out to be a productive citizen after all.

Have you had any experiences where you were under pressure to handle something big, but you weren't quite sure whether you did the right thing? The best part about looking behind us is that we can view the past calmly, see the steps we took, and how they affected the situation. And we can determine what we could do better in the future. A leader under fire makes mistakes, but a growing leader will learn from those teachers who appeared and be ready for the next set of circumstances to handle.

At the entrance to a refugee camp, I noticed a man throwing rocks at us. But being focused on my assignment, I didn't pay attention to him. My mistake. I should have read the telltale signs better and gone to a different camp that day. My mistake nearly cost me my life that day.

We drove into the camp and began to walk among the people who were suffering from the terrible living conditions there. My team carried the provisions we were going to give away up to a tent that had been temporarily set up for mothers and babies to rest beneath. We parked the car at the end of the camp and started walking the rocky area littered with garbage from the hastily set up refugee areas. I noticed there were no latrines here, only an open air, narrow ditch that ran the camp's length. I didn't pay attention to the gathering men who began to follow me. I focused on the crying babies and moms weeping with exhaustion and need whom I was passing.

When I got to the tent, I immediately started passing out supplies, food, and simple medical provisions for the moms there. I held the babies and talked to the moms about caring for them. I was putting ointment and Band-Aids on the skinned knees of toddlers when suddenly I noticed that men were starting to press into the tent, and they were talking loudly. Mothers backed up with their babies and melted into the background, leaving me to face an angry mob of men who instantly became aggressive toward me.

I look around for my interpreter, only to find that she had run away, leaving me to face this angry group without any way to communicate with them. The team with me, running the camera and in charge of the supplies, stood frozen and in complete silence. I wasn't quite sure what to do…but I realized that the wrong thing could start a physical fight and we could be hurt or killed.

Suddenly, I remembered the guy throwing rocks at our vehicle. Too late now to heed that warning. The only words I could make out from their screams was "President Clinton" and "food." I realized they thought I was part of an American government aid office, and they were demanding to know why they hadn't been given the money being raised to help them. I brought out the Moms Against Hunger brochures about the food we were giving away to show them who I was. They promptly threw the brochures on the ground, increasing the tension. I knew I could not get them to understand anything in the state of mind they were in.

Leaders must empathize with those who are frustrated with what is happening in their lives. All I had to do was look around at the shambles they were living in to understand how frustrated they must be. Having left their homes and all normalcy of life, they were now forced to live outdoors on a rocky hillside with no outside help at all. No food, no water, no latrines, no beds even to sleep in. I was the first helper they had seen, but I represented the lack of care, abuse of others, and endless miles of red tape by huge organizations that had promised help that hadn't arrived. I could understand how they felt, and if it had been me in this condition, I would have been mad too.

I was there to help them, but it was too little and too late in their minds. Because I understood how they felt, they did not offend me with their anger. I said an SOS prayer under my breath and did what next came to my mind. The best I could do now was to look like I was listening to their ranting shouts, keep eye contact, smile with assurance, use body language to quiet them, and show them I had brought them help. But I was too far away from our vehicle if something tipped them over the edge. So I just slipped into 'Mom" mode. Threatening doesn't work when kids are too old (and these were), so I took charge of everyone by candy! I took control as if they were all my kids.

I told my frozen team to smile at them and to get out the suckers we had brought for the children. With one accord, everyone put down their backpacks, dug out their bags of candy, and immediately started passing them out.

I figured it would be harder for these men to yell with suckers in their mouths. And it might buy me a little time to calm down the situation. The angry men readily took the suckers, and without thinking, they opened them and put them in their mouths. Sudden silence. Despite glaring looks still on their faces, they all had sticks coming out of their mouths and were standing there like big distracted kids. Good.

So I smiled brightly at them and told them I had presents for everyone. Using hand motions, I encouraged them all to come with me. My team urgently said between their clamped teeth and fake smiles, "What are you doing?" I said back, smiling without looking at them, "We are going back to our vehicle, and they are coming with us. Everybody wave at them to come with us."

Slowly, the mob understood that I had something for them, and to get it, they had to come with me. So now, instead of me running away from them, which would have ended with a mob mentality taking over and us getting killed, they were walking with me. I was trying to figure out who was the leader of this bunch while we walked and they hopefully calmed down. My team kept passing out suckers as the men finished them. I motioned the entire way with my hands for them to keep coming with me. The leader revealed himself to me through his fast orders to everyone to follow.

When we reached the vehicle, I saw my hired interpreter locked inside. I could understand why everyone was so upset and I could even feel their pain, but when I saw my interpreter, who had been hired to be my communication, locked in the car, I made an executive decision that as soon as we were back in a safe zone, she would be fired. Not only had she put the lives of the entire team at great risk, but she hadn't told me what was being said the whole time I was walking to the tent. She had just left.

Leaders under fire never leave their teams behind.

I made the interpreter get out of the vehicle with a smiling threat in my voice. I had her interpret for me with a scared smile on her face. I had her tell the mob's leader to come and stand in the middle of the group and to have everyone else back up around him. The mob of men were mystified, but they still had suckers in their mouths, so they were quiet and followed my instructions. Their body language—spread legs and folded arms—said to me, "We are still very much antagonistic toward you, and you better have something good for us!"

I then told my team to unload from the vehicle all of our supplies we had packed for the day. Our lives were worth more than the provisions we had, and I wanted to make sure we made a big enough presentation to distract the mob for a few minutes. Mutely, my team obeyed, and I directed all the goods to be piled up around the mob leader's feet. Immediately, the people tried to push forward to get the supplies, but I told them we were making a big presentation, and they needed to wait till the speech was over.

So everything got piled around the leader and piled into his arms as well. I told my team, "Make it as much as he can hold," and I kept everyone back by walking around with a smile and handing out more suckers to them. I felt like Vanna White on a game show! By now, about one hundred were in the mob and there were only five of us. When the vehicle was completely empty, I instructed my team to get in the vehicle, leave the front doors open, and to start the vehicle.

With me holding the interpreter's hand so she would not run again, I assured her we were all going to be okay now. And with her help, I told the leader that we had brought help to their camp because we cared and we wanted to show support for the suffering they were going through. The big, big surprise was that everything we had was all for them, and *on the count of three*, they could all get what they wanted from the big guy in the middle. He was trying to look at me over the pile of provisions that filled his arms. He was feeling special; it hadn't yet dawned on him what was about to happen to him. Maybe the taste of sugar still in his mouth had disconnected his anger for the moment. It took a minute for the interpreter to go through "1...2...3!"

When "3!" was said, the crowd turned on their leader and began to pull, struggle, and grab for anything they could. Momentarily forgotten in the frenzy, the interpreter and I jumped in the vehicle, slammed it into gear, and raced out of there!

No one in the vehicle said anything. There was complete *dead silence*. I turned around in the front seat and burst out laughing as I looked at everyone. I really don't know what happened to the mob after we left that day, but I learned several valuable lessons:

211

1. A leader under fire must empathize with those who are in a greater position of control if she is going to get the control away from them.

2. Even angry adults still have an inner child that can be reached by a leader who uses respect.

3. A leader under fire can draw instant wisdom from a quick prayer and the following idea that comes.

4. A leader under fire needs an interpreter who has steady nerves.

5. A leader under fire has to have a sense of humor to lighten up tension.

I think that day all the mentors in my life must have come out at once. First of all, I believe the Holy Spirit gave me the idea for how to handle this volatile situation on the spot. Then Nona Freeman, Pauline Gruse, Else Lund, and Sam Latta all came out in me in that hour of living on the edge!

What was my mistake? I should have paid better attention to the man throwing rocks at me. He was telling me not to come in, but I didn't listen. Lesson learned.

QUESTIONS TO PONDER:

1. In a tough time in your leadership, were there any signals you missed along the way that were hints to guide you?

_____

_____

_____

_____

2. What would be your "courage under fire" statements that you learned?

_____

_____

_____

_____

18

Standing in the Shoes of Empathy

When a poor person dies of hunger, it has not happened because God did not take care of him or her. It has happened because neither you nor I wanted to give that person what he or she needed.
— Mother Teresa

My stories here are just a few of the mistakes I have made under fire. I'm sure that you can add some of your own in this journey called life that we are both living. The growing leader will understand his or her lessons and not forget what was captured in the process so he or she can become a better leader down the road. Your work as a leader at home, or in your business, your marriage, your childrearing, and even your faith will all require that you learn from the past the clear lessons to climb to higher purposes and to greater assignments in life.

Our responsible actions in the pressure cookers of life open the way ahead for greater abilities, opportunities, and projects. We all know that no one can exactly know how our life feels because that person is not walking in our shoes. But with empathy, we can use the experiences of life itself to show us how others have to walk and live.

WALKING IN THEIR SHOES

I outgrew my shoes. My younger brothers had no trouble with this issue because they could simply grow into their older brother Alan's shoes. But there was no one to share shoes with me. And before long, I was out of shoes. On his busy trips to other missions, villages, and towns, my dad would hunt for a pair for me to wear. And upon his return trips, Mother would always ask, "Did you find any shoes for Gayla?" None could be found.

In Fassama, it was very important for us to have shoes because of the constant threat of snakes, bugs, and bacteria, in and on the ground. So it became a concern to my parents for me to have protection on my feet! My parents wrote back to the States to their family and friends, asking for shoes for me. I remember Mother putting paper under my feet and having me stand on it so she could draw an outline of my feet to send with her request to the U.S. "Please send Gayla a pair of shoes. We cannot find anything here to fit her." None came.

Finally, my dad managed to find a pair of shoes for me. They were secondhand, but given by a kind person at the embassy in Monrovia. But I didn't care. Finally...shoes! And when Dad went to get them... the shoes turned out to be a pair of used Dr. Scholl's wooden sandals with a dark blue strap over the toes and a buckle to keep them tight. I was happy; they felt good! The cool curved wood under my bare feet felt relaxing, yet firm. Mother was not so pleased because my feet would be exposed—but what else could we do? I ended up wearing those shoes for almost two years! They were my only pair. I wore them to church, to school, out to play, to bathe, literally everywhere! I loved clomping them and making my steps as noisy as possible. Funny, the wooden bases never wore out and somehow they fit my growing feet all that time!

Finally, we got an eagerly awaited package from America! It was always like Christmas when we would receive something from the good old U.S.A. Everyone gathered around as the package was carefully opened; we hoped whatever was inside was not damaged and would be something we really could use.

It was a pair of shoes for Gayla Joyce! A little pair of cute, black and white Oxfords…. I was thrilled! And promptly, I sat down to try the pretty little shoes on, only to be so very disappointed. They were too small. How could this be? Finally, I had gotten real shoes…. It seemed like a cruel joke to me. My disappointment could only be expressed in tears. What could my parents say? They too were unhappy about it. But shoes were a premium, so we could not afford to ignore this gift.

So my parents decided, "Hey, shoes are shoes, and we have other children. These shoes will not go to waste." So it was decided that my youngest brother, Regan, would try them on. And to his dismay I am sure, the cute little girl shoes fit him. The other two brothers were ordered in no uncertain terms that they would not be making remarks of *any kind* about Regan's new shoes.

So Regan got a new pair of girly shoes and I continued wearing my old wooden clog sandals. Somehow, we all outgrew those days of childhood, and eventually, I got a pair of clear plastic "jellies" from an Indian store in a town.

This experience taught me to look at the shoes on other people's feet. African feet were dusty and tough from never having shoes on. Shoes to the Africans represented wealth. Their small children could not run and play freely because their feet would be tender on the rocks…. Baby feet would be easily cut on sharp rocks, and getting an infection is so easy in the wild. It would take a while before a tough callous would literally cover the bottoms of their feet, protecting them with their own skin.

I still know how it feels to be a child and be handed a pair of shoes… maybe your first pair ever. To sit down to try them on with eyes dancing…only to find they don't fit and you can't force them onto your feet. I can clearly see the heart-hitting disappointment in their eyes whenever I give a pair of shoes only to find that they do not fit. I feel the same regret in my heart as theirs. But their sweet manners persist and they don't say anything. No complaints, no crying—a hard life has taught them that they cannot have what their eyes want. And they would never want me to think the shoes meant that much to them…. Yet I see…and I know…and the law of the wild is that they all know not to embarrass the one trying to help them. But their politeness is also a pain to me because I know what is clearly happening in their little hearts. And it's still disappointment.

I have picked up many children and looked at their shoes to see how their parents have cut out the toes so they could keep wearing them. There are real reasons why a child can be without a single pair of shoes to wear:

1. Not having the funds to buy a pair.

2. No transportation to get to a town to find a pair.

3. No shoes available to buy.

Sometimes people look at the downtrodden and think, "Why don't they just find something better to do with their lives, go live someplace else, just get their kids in school somewhere. Just get out of *there?*"

Sadly in developing countries, there is no someplace else, some other school, some other life for them to run and grab ahold of. Because of various reasons such as the lack of a stable economy, the two classes of people—rich and poor—may live where there are no existing schools, no medical care available, and no job opportunities. Without transportation, their worlds become very small. Environmental issues—such as being in a tropical jungle where only a few items will grow well, famines, floods, tsunamis, and earthquakes—plus wars and government corruption are all factors that affect the lives of those born in such countries.

The compassionate care of leaders—who understand these issues, empathize with people affected by them, and bring aid to struggling families—is the only thing that will make a difference. *Pain teaches us to empathize, but it's up to us to remember the lesson and use it to better mankind.*

QUESTIONS TO PONDER:

1. A growing leader's heart will open as a result of understanding pain personally. How has your heart opened by reading this book?

_____

_____

_____

_____

2. Advocacy for the helpless is…. (Write your own definition here.)

_____

_____

_____

_____

19

Knocking on the
Door of Chance

God gives nothing to those who keep their arms crossed.
— African Proverb

DOORWAYS OF POSSIBILITY

The leader within you will flourish and grow when you have mentors around you. This book will now serve as one of the mentors in your library to use as a resource for understanding and empathizing with the needs of others. I hope to enlarge your heart to reach out and become a humanitarian for the nations in need. You have had many leaders in your life along the way, both the positive and the negative, for it takes both types to give us balance and clear do's and don'ts to follow. But sometimes we don't recognize people as mentors because they don't announce themselves as such to us. They just begin to shape us….

Your leadership will begin to show in the lives of other people too. Have you empathized with others in the past? Given advice or been a sounding board for someone who trusted you for direction? Or maybe you are just beginning to see how you can be an influencer and make a positive impact on someone else's life? It is rewarding and fulfilling to see others follow in your footsteps and take on your mission as their own.

Finding the right projects to be involved with is like opening the important doors that change our lives for the better. You will open doors to blessings both by offering aid as a leader who assists others in need and from those whom you have helped. People, circumstances, or opportunities can be doors we find to open.

OPENING DOORS FROM THE INSIDE

Our family has an amazing artifact from the West African jungle village where we lived. This vintage treasure is an actual door to an African hut that is mounted on a wall. It's about 5' x 3' and heavily carved; it's one solid thick slab of wood.

The top and bottom still have the wooden, carved hinge pins used to hang the door on the mud, thatched roof hut. Actual huts have small doorways through which one has to bend down to enter. The door's latch is on the left and is still in perfect order. The carvings are of hunters with crocodiles and spears. It's a very special piece, and it's very unique to own it privately.

An African man was running through the mission in Fassama and carrying this large door on his back. When he recognized that he was on a mission, he stopped and offered it to my dad. We suspect he had been involved in attacking a nearby village and had stolen this valuable door, which might have belonged to a chief's hut because of the detailed carvings. No other warriors came out of the bush with him, so it was impossible to find out the story behind it. If he was part of an attacking tribe, the rest of the tribe simply melted back into the jungle and no one ever knew. We could not find out who it belonged to, and since the man was tired of carrying this massive carved piece that had no value to him, it became ours.

Someone of importance lost this beautifully carved door, and maybe his life, in whatever drama had happened. In those days, without any government protection, no police presence, or any other form of protection, everyone was at the mercy of everyone else.

Greed can make a theft look good, until one has to carry the load of guilt.

All we had for protection was God and His angels, who always stood guard around us. No one *ever* attacked our base while we lived there. So this door stands as a testimony and a treasured family heirloom to our family of God's care over us. The door of protection was always locked shut against evil in our family.

THE DOORS OF CHANCE

This beautiful door represents the door of chance to me. Chances are endless before our feet. Which doors should you open and which ones should you just silently walk past? Many decisions must be made every day in the life of a leader. Should we call this person? Should we stop by here? Do I decide to rule on this matter today? Choices come our way constantly; some are nothing but distractions and some turn out to be hindrances, but there are also those doors that are really perfect for you, though in the beginning, they are just doors of chance.

Passageways that lead to other connections, people, and opportunities are very important because they either lead you further down the road of your mission, or they take you down someone else's road and dilute your own momentum in your mission. These doorways can and should be tested, but not walked through quickly without knowledge. *There is a big difference between knocking on a door and someone knocking on your door.* The deliberate reason for both can be vastly different.

WHEN THE DOOR SLAMS SHUT

Sometimes, doors slam shut abruptly, making us change the course we are on. After physically working ten long years and making many sacrifices to build our dream church, warehouse, and home, we were within twelve months of completion. Having planned how to build this unique and special green building that would be protected from cold winters in Bloomington, Illinois, our years had been spent working, developing, and gathering the "green" materials to build our dream operation.

But one day it all changed, bringing destruction and abrupt change to us. It snowed extra heavily one late afternoon and long into the night. The next morning when we awoke, the weight of the snow had collapsed critical parts of our building! We were in shock and speechless that this had happened. All the years…all the money… all our sacrifice had been wiped out. Again, an agent of change had visited us and we had to focus sharply to make instant decisions. Heartbroken and devastated, it was hard for us to know what to do next!

And we were forced to go through a door we did not want to go through—letting our vision die. We had to leave with a truck packed with our life's belongings and many personal buckets of searing hot tears. And we had to recognize that the reasons we had worked so hard were not so important—we as people were. Our lives counted, and the years we had spent building our dream we would not get back again, although the wisdom we gained would benefit us greatly down life's road. It's not the "Why?" that matters—it's the "Now what?" that does. A deepened leader adjusts his sails and carries on.

Every truly great leader throughout history has had to go through the doors of failure over and over to learn stamina, fortitude, outstanding courage, incredible creativity, audacity, resilience, resourcefulness, and daring nerve. *Winning does not teach the greatest lessons in a leader's life...failure does.* Why? Because there is a particular destiny that only a single person is being prepared for—and it took every door of failure to prepare that person well for that single date with destiny to change nations.

Look at the life of forceful President Abraham Lincoln; he suffered through eight election failures before his leadership changed America and broke the curse of slavery from her feet. Door after door slammed in his face before the right one opened, and when it did, he was ready for the battle to change the nation.

See the life of Sir Winston Churchill and see the string of failures behind him and the massive assignment that this mighty man was ordained to undertake as a leader to break the back of Hitler's terror at long last.

View the giant of a man named President Nelson Mandela who went through twenty-seven years of prison before breaking the nation of South Africa into a new era, forever changing her destiny.

Life's doors bring change to every person who crosses the thresholds of action. Doors that we pass through have the invisible law of cause and effect in place. Action and reaction. It's wise to take into account all the areas of change that will occur by going through a door. In leadership, it's called "counting the cost."

Your leadership skills will be honed by experience. And experience will develop into wisdom. And wisdom will lead you past many a door that hides a blank wall. The secret will be to remember the doors you are passing or opening as the maze to a successful future.

Regret says, "Oh, if only I hadn't gone through that door!"

But Wisdom says, "We have learned much and won't have to go in that door again."

Thomas Edison was one such special person who kept knocking on all the ideas and doors that he came to. Most didn't open, but stubbornly, he kept knocking. In time, he was fired from early jobs because he was told he wasn't working hard enough. In spite of all discouragements, he went on to unlock the doors of the lightbulb, which changed the world. The phonograph and the motion picture camera would also change the world. He was one single person who refused to quit knocking until he found doors that would open.

Everyone has an inner map that may not match yours and a door doesn't necessarily mean direction. But sometimes you have to open a door, put your head inside, and look around for a minute to see whether it could be a match. And sometimes, delightfully, it is.

QUESTIONS TO PONDER:

1. What doors have you opened that have led you to a higher rate of success?

_____

_____

_____

2. What is the next door in front of you that you are sure is the right one?

_____

_____

_____

3. As a leader, what doors will you tell those following you not to enter?

_____

_____

_____

4. What doors will you open for others following you?

_____

_____

_____

5. Have you ever entered a door that you didn't plan to, and what did you learn from that experience?

_____

_____

_____

6. What is the name of a great leader who inspired you to be more than you ever were before?

_____

_____

_____

7. What was it in that person's life that ignited your heart in a new way?

_____

_____

_____

20

Passion Fuels Energy

I believe that if you show people the problems and you show them the solutions, they will be moved to act.
— Bill Gates

THINKING OUTSIDE THE BOX

You have uncovered twenty principles to grow the leader within you that can help you to grow in your life, your work, and your faith. Seeing these principles through the sum total of your life adventures can cause your passion to excel in greater measures. I have discovered that my passion to reach out to people spurs my energy on, which causes me to reach higher to complete my goals. What a person is passionate about will be what he spends his time on. That energy will be reflected in his leadership style in life, work, and faith.

Listed below are creative solutions that result from the passion to help people and the energy fueled by that passion. Creative ideas that leaders implement trigger greater solutions in all kinds of situations to help people in need. These are ways to help solve local and world problems. Be the kind of leader who is solution-oriented when faced with problems. As you read of ways others have solved problems with creative solutions, ideas will come to you that you can implement. Every solution began with the energy of a leader being fueled by his or her personal passion.

In impoverished nations, there are only two classes of people: the rich and the poor. You are either one or the other. The rich are focused on staying rich, while the poor have no advocates to lift them from the depths of poverty. Finding solutions for the poor must include, within each nation, ways for the poor to sell to the rich or provide services that will sustain them. There is no dignity in just receiving handouts. Leaders look for ways to cause the poor and unfortunate to become self-sustainable and independent for life. A few successful examples I have seen are:

1. Local houses that are turned into homes for both orphaned children and elderly, destitute people thrown away by society. Localized systems have created housing for both the young and old under the same roof, and together, they provide support for each other. The elder teach the younger about life, the responsibilities of growing up, cooking, and caring for the young. The younger teach the elder that they still have purpose and are loved while also providing the energetic arms and legs for the daily work. People who had been thrown away find purpose living together. Children, who have suffered the loss of their parents, through the suffering of diseases like HIV, find comfort in the arms of a lonely older person.

2. Creating vegetable gardens along with chickens, goats, and a cow for milking. These types of home "farms" can become self-sustainable once begun. The extra vegetables, eggs, and livestock are sold alongside the roads, helping to provide for the people's needs.

3. Sewing centers that teach the skill of sewing with the old fashioned pedal sewing machines that do not require electricity. Once having been taught, people are able to create clothing, bags, backpacks, and various other cloth items such as rugs, tablemats, and runners. These are sold in markets.

4. The skill of carving handmade wooden pieces is a great talent and should be encouraged as a way of personal provision. Leaders provide ideas for different objects for the people to create since variety helps to sell a larger number of goods to passing people.

5. Co-ops where various different craftsmen join together to provide a market of sorts for all of their wares to be displayed. These co-ops can provide solid income for a family in need.

6. Specialty farms such as coffee farms or catfish farms that grow specific things for business owners around the world.

7. Industrious people live around the world; they only need the ideas or to be shown how to create a solution to assist them in becoming independent in life. What they have readily available sometimes is nothing but rags, old worn clothing, pieces of tree branches, shells, leaves, and branches, or clay soil, rocks, and the odd piece of trash or board. Out of these items, industrious people are making baskets, jewelry, rugs, grass mats, clay pots, and carved pieces.

8. Portable water purifiers are used to provide the life-sustaining pure water to cook and wash with. A portable water purifier can also be used to sell water in the markets, providing income for an individual, or a church or school to provide for its students.

9. Used clothing is used to help people become their own small businesses. Each micro-enterprise can be started with a small amount of clothing.

10. Training in handcrafted crochet items made out of yarn and thread become saleable to tourists. Small dresses, shawls, scarves, hats, baby items, tablecloths, and other common products can all be created to provide income.

11. Mobile food carts that cook where people gather or commute become the foundation for a restaurant.

12. Craftsmen can produce rugs from rags and turn palm branches into floor mats.

HOW CAN I HELP?

Become a part of the ongoing solutions to help families in need. Through these simple measures, you can be involved in becoming a humanitarian. Being a philanthropist who finds significance in helping to change the world can be done right at home by using your leadership skills. Find a passion that will fuel your energy! Don't try to talk people down on their prices. Sales of their products is what they are living on, and your purchase may be the only income they make for the week.

1. Donate your used goods of all sorts to worthy organizations; you can find their *actual ongoing efforts* easily on websites. Their needs include clothing, shoes, belts, purses, hats, dishes, pots and pans, house wares, linens, rugs and mats, small pictures, and knickknacks. **www.ProjectGlobalFashion.org** or **www.RoleModelsofAmerica.org**

2. Support Moms Against Hunger and become a partner with other mothers around the world to effect change for mothers raising children in poverty stricken nations worldwide. **www. MomsAgainstHunger.org**

3. Start adding worth to our charity work by spreading the news. Help your friends and family to learn about the ongoing work through social media such as Facebook: Moms Against Hunger.

4. Share ongoing projects by your own communications in technology, such as online Websites, Blogs, Twitter, Facebook, emails, texts, and faxes.

5. Host charity events for the specific projects, and plan a support goal to reach.

6. Make financial giving a part of your life and become a monthly financial partner to provide consistent support to help. Find the "Donate" button on the front page and become an automatic donor every month. **www.MomsAgainstHunger.org**

7. Network with civic groups to raise awareness among others to help.

8. Do presentations to groups, teens, schools, and businesses to provide support for the charity.

9. Be a leader and speak up for the underprivileged. Make it part of your business or employment to care about those in needs. Put Moms Against Hunger as a charity on the list for corporate sponsors.

10. Become a pipeline of supply for others by shipping goods to schools, churches, hospitals, and missionaries. Support their efforts by what you send to them.

QUESTIONS TO PONDER:

1. As a leader, how do you intend to add value to the world around you?

_____

_____

_____

_____

2. What will be your method and area to work on?

_____

_____

_____

_____

3. Who can be on your team to help you accomplish your goal to help?

_____

_____

_____

_____

Passion fuels energy,
causing leaders to go beyond themselves
to stay later, work harder, to provide lasting love and support
to truly help someone
impoverished outside of their control.
— Gayla Holley

A Window on the World

This book has been written to teach you as a growing leader how to apply the lessons that life is teaching you and how to become an incredible leader for others as a result. All of the written history here is to remind us that we live in a world of need.

My personal faith in Jesus Christ and His salvation for me is what started me on the road toward helping people in need. My faith is the sustaining underpinning of my life. I hope and trust that you too will come to know Him as your Lord and Savior.

Your future is bright with new ideas, great significance, and incredible opportunities ahead. Now that you have seen so many facets of life outside of your own, you as a leader have to decide four things about yourself and your future.

1. Are you a mirror or a window?

   As a mirror, we can merely reflect like a mirror does what's going on in the world and choose only to mirror the needs, but do nothing as a responsible world citizen to bring answers to fix the human needs. The title of Humanitarian means nothing without the actual proof of work being done. We might have the "look" of doing good around the world, but in reality, only use empty promotions through others as a deflecting reflection.

2. Are you a window?

    Windows are to see out of; they can be lifted up and reached out through, but they are not meant to be used as an actual door through which to go somewhere. As a window, we see the need from afar and could maybe help if our emotions were touched just right and we feel the desire to give impulsively at the moment.

3. Do you look *at* the window, or do you look *through* the window at the scene happening right outside our personal lives?

    Maybe some would like to look at the problems and talk about them, but they haven't yet decided to jump in and start doing something personally to change things.

4. Will you look *through* the window to see the need and then go to a door to do something about it?

    There are those who have been told about the needs of humanity, see the window, walk over to it, and carefully look through the window at the needs outside. Take the time to see what stands just outside this modern world in need, and then makes a conscious decision to go to a door and do something to change it.... That person is a humanitarian world leader, and this book will help him or her to grow into a mighty tree that will shade many thousands of lives.

Look through the windowpanes...at the history of this book. Can you see the many thin and hungry children still surrounding us at this present time? Just a short 2-3 hour plane trip from Houston, Texas are mothers in Latin America who are still carrying huge loads of sticks on their heads to provide warmth and fire to cook with for their children. Their weary lives have been lived like this for centuries.

Look across to Africa…. Can you see the tall, painfully thin women scratching in the dirt, looking for roots, a forgotten cassava, something…anything to eat. Can you see the flattened and dried breasts that have no milk to feed their babies in places like Mali?

Look through the window at Haiti…. Life is forever tough there for a mother and child in need….

Sir Winston Churchill said these words that marked me:

> ***You make a living by what you get….***
> ***You make a life by what you give.***

Peer through the windows at the refugee camps in Pakistan—at the women sitting dejectedly on stumps in the sun, hopeless from the increasing wars going on around them.

See the raw shed in Guatemala where I was taken once to pray for a dying mother who could go no further in life.

Examine the orphans in Romania through the tearful watery panes of glass; they would have given anything to be able to come home with me to live.

I see again the little mom standing just beyond my window who has just returned from the hospital where her baby, now held fiercely in her arms, was in the hospital for pneumonia from living in such wet and moldy conditions, and now she's back in the same hovel. She needs someone to bring bleach and teach her about what the mold is doing, but she has never been to school and simply does not know. She needs a mentor mother to teach her….

Unwanted, unloved, uncared for, and forgotten—the orphans of the world who have no mothers need our care. Pakistan, along with other impoverished nations, is asking Moms Against Hunger to send aid to its thrown away children.... We hope to send aid soon.

See the handicapped people who crawl along the ground because there are no agencies to help them, no possible way to get a wheelchair. We project that we will lift the handicapped from the ground and put them in our smiley carts with dignity.

Watch the South American nations in this hemisphere that are starving, living in absolute squalor and misery. It's not looking at the massive problems that require impossibilities that we need to focus on, but rather seeing small villages, and pueblos, and kraals where together with partners, we can truly help.

A window of action always begins with finding a need and filling it. A woman *can* make a difference in the world—children depend on a mother to care for them.

Women are the greatest untapped natural resource on planet earth. Motivating women to become the leaders needed on the earth is a window on my world. Mothers in Africa…Mothers in Asia… Mothers in India…Mothers in America…Mothers in Canada…ALL can see a greater purpose for their lives when they look through the **window of action.**

Throw open your windows…. See the world I am showing you. Your life can most certainly make a difference to someone in need.

You can see out of a window of financial provision for those you love around you, plus a view of significance…of helping the helpless from your business. Look through the window of opportunity and see how big your world can be. See the smiling faces and hands reaching for the supplies you have brought them. See the children grab you to hug you in gratitude!

> *Let us touch the dying...the poor...the lonely...the hungry...*
> *the unwanted...according to the graces we have received...*
> *and let us not be ashamed or slow to do the humble work.*
> — Mother Teresa

Moms Against Hunger ships container loads of rice meals filled with vitamins, minerals, protein, amino acids, and rice! It's a far better product to reach a far greater number of families. It's our turn now as women to help shape the world...you and I...can feed hungry children.... Right now.

> *Make it a personal rule...never to lie down at night without being*
> *able to say, "I have fed hungry children and made their little*
> *lives better this day.*
> — Gayla Holley

You can join in, and together, we can add value to thousands of lives. Have you ever said in your mind, "I wish I could do something about this need"? Here is your chance....

Provision...Partners...Passion—with these three things I plan to change lives.

It's the window on my world.

The 20 Guidelines for Work, Life, and Faith

Life's adventures and challenges have been my teachers in numerous ways. With expectations of a life spent living a dream, I have learned that destiny has certain principles that, if followed, will allow the journey to become more understandable and accepted. Here are the traits I have uncovered that will help you on your journey toward fulfilling your dreams. Going forward after reading this book, I hope you will begin to look for how the leadership points I've discussed will be uncovered in each of your life experiences. You have many stories of your own experiences that you could add to each chapter. Look inward at your life to see whether you may find a pathway similar to mine! The twenty traits listed below are single sentence confessions of *Growing the Leader Within You*. You will find them to be proven principles for leadership in life, work, and your faith.

1. I will learn to ask the Right Question in life's unexpected sudden turns.

2. My destiny is like a puzzle with pieces that fit together and make a beautiful picture.

3. I will let go of the familiar as part of the process of stepping into the future.

4. I accept that living the new dream will not be like living in the past.

5. I will choose mentors along the way to help guide me.

6. My mind map will need to be adjusted.

7. Answers will be found right in front of me as they are uncovered by time and circumstance.

8. I will watch over little details daily, which will yield big results.

9. I will find unusual friendships that offer support for my destiny.

10. I will develop my communication and coordination skills.

11. I will identify my personal coaches.

12. I will honor my personal history.

13. I will develop determination because giving up is not an option.

14. I will turn my desperation into creativity.

15. I will learn to give out of my need.

16. I will dream with my eyes wide open.

17. I will train so I will have courage under fire.

18. I will stand in the shoes of empathy for others.

19. I will knock on the door of chance.

20. I will remember that my passion will fuel my energy.

How many of the leadership principles in *Growing the Leader Within You* have also led you? Have they become strong underpinnings beneath your life as a leader? You have the power as a leader to offer significant help to others in need. Do you practice these principles often? Look back over these guidelines and study the stories beneath the surface to gain a deeper understanding of the principles. Live a life that counts for the good of others. You have received so much in life to offer others, and you have earned an enhanced, valued place of leadership from which to provide solutions.

The Compassionate Humanitarian's Creed

1. I will seek to use my faith in compassionate endeavors.

2. I will seek to use my leadership skills to help those in poverty.

3. I will be a responsible world citizen to create solutions.

4. I will develop a clear vision, making a difference in the lives of those living in the developing world.

5. When opportunity to help comes, I will confidently offer my support.

6. I will begin a personal project to bring about change for the betterment of other people.

7. I will not quit or turn away from those in need, but recognize that in time, my capabilities will increase, giving me a better way to assist through my project.

8. I will prove that opposition can be overcome.

9. I will complete each project because I have what it takes as a leader to plan, lead, execute, and develop a lasting change.

10. I am a humanitarian, caring for others…this is who I am.

About the Author

Gayla was born in Benton, Illinois to Sam and Joyce Latta. Adventure came early as a tornado ripped through the small town of Benton, Illinois when Gayla was only eight days old. With Gayla cradled in her father's arms, the young family knelt in prayer beside a closet when the house was blown away, leaving only their lives intact.

At age seven, Gayla moved with her parents and three brothers to Liberia, West Africa, sixty-five miles from the nearest motor road in a mud house located central to a jungle village. Along with her brothers, Gayla attended school taught by her mother. The experience of this early adventure provided her with an early education in humanitarian mission work, which impacted her for life.

Upon return to the United States to complete schooling, Gayla met and married Evangelist Gregory Holley on December 27, 1975. As itinerant ministers and teachers, they have traveled throughout the world and continue to do so as Ambassadors of New Life Foundation. Their ministry is in many nations where they educate, feed, and bring medicine and clothing to those less fortunate.

Gayla birthed their baby girl, Angela, in Harare, Zimbabwe, during the civil war of Rhodesia while they were missionaries there. She also home-schooled their daughter for ten years.

Supporting orphanages for hurting children, and homes for those in poverty, Dr. Gayla's compassion for the young encircles the world. She founded the organization **Moms Against Hunger**, which annually feeds hundreds of thousands of children and their mothers around the world. Moms Against Hunger assists others in setting up food pantries to provide for local communities, as well as offers aid in disasters for earthquake victims, hurricanes, floods, fires, and tornados in the U.S.

Millions of packages of formulated rice meals have been distributed in many nations to provide essential nutrients, vitamins, minerals, and vital nourishment to the starving through Dr. Gayla's efforts. Zimbabwe, Pakistan, Ghana, Liberia, Mexico, Romania, Belize, Malawi, Haiti, Guatemala, Fiji, Honduras, Zambia, and Mauritius are just a few of the list of nations where containers of aid have been shipped to provide food and supplies to the impoverished. Please visit **www.MomsAgainstHunger.org** to see ongoing efforts in different nations. Or join us at Facebook/Moms Against Hunger.

Dr. Gayla founded **Role Models of America** to encourage women who succeed to model and lead the next generation. The program is designed to allow women to use their abilities and talents to fulfill the desire to help others. She has hosted many educational events helping women to achieve personal life skills and leadership. She manages the Role Models of America Thrift Store which serves the working poor with vouchers for needs. **www.RoleModelsofAmerica.org**

Dr. Gayla serves on the Advisory Board of **Project Global Fashion** **www.ProjectGlobalFashion.com** which provides sustainable micro-enterprise in Third World nations.

She is the Founder of the **Pass it On Program** at Illinois State University.

She is a singer and original songwriter for two recordings: "Sanctuary" and "Reflecting Your Glory."

She was the dramatist, playwright, and producer of *The Big Bang*, *The Mysterious Woman*, *The Razor's Edge*, *The Bag Lady*, *Baby Baby*, *Equipped But Not Prepared*, and *The Experience*.

The following are a partial list of her teaching projects: New Horizons for Women, Time Management for Women, the Love Scrapbook, The Successful Working Woman's Guide, The HomeBuilder Series, The Worship Leaders Manual, and Pro31.

She is a writer for the Community Bible Institute, which has over 1,600 incarcerated men and women enrolled in forty-three states whom her writings encourage. She has many years of teaching and training through lessons, seminars, and classes for women in leadership.

SPECIAL HONORS, CERTIFICATES, AND AWARDS:

- She is one of the Thousand Points of Light in America. In 1991, Dr. Gayla, along with her husband, was awarded #389 in President George W. Bush's 1000 Points of Light.

- Dr. Gayla has received numerous awards for her community service and her advocacy for women and children and was nominated as the "The Woman of Distinction" for the Ten Top Women in Houston, Texas in 2005.

- Awarded Dame of Grace by the Sovereign Order of Saint John of Jerusalem, Knights of Malta, Ecumenical Order.

- Awarded Commemorative Medal in Recognition for her Charities by H.S.H. The Grand Master, Count Joseph Frendo Combo CD, GB, GCSJ(H), MOC, ORCB, D.Hum, Ph.D., Marquis & Count de Torre Sarroca, Grand Bailiff, Grand Cross of Justice, Hereditary Knight, the Knights Hospitallers, OSJ.

- She received the Service Recognition Award from the Houston Police Department for her work and aid to Haiti in 2010.

- She serves beside her husband, who is the Metropolitan Archbishop and President of Independent Christian Churches International, which serves over 4,500 men and women across America in Pastoral Ministry.

- She has her own blog **www.GaylasMagazine.com** and writes on different facets of leadership, travel, family, education, and faith. She has touched over 100,000 readers who follow her online.

EDUCATION:

- Certificate of Ordination – 1984

- Illinois State University – 1987 Senior Counselor for Women's Crisis Centers

- Dame of Grace of The Knights of Malta – 1998

- The Therapon Institute Licensed Pastoral Counselor – 2003

- The Therapon Institute Belief Therapist – 2003

- Light Learning Institute – Extraordinary Women Course – AACC 2003

- American Association of Christian Counselors – Member since 2005

- Doctor of Divinity Degree – 2009 American Bible College

- Served as an Executive Board Member of The Bridge – a Shelter for Battered Women

- Facilitator and Teacher of many Marriage Classes

- Houston Police Department – Certificate of Training for Profiling Criminal Behavior

- Served as a Senior Counselor for the Women's Crisis Centers – Illinois State University

- Certificate of Appreciation by the American Bible Society

- Certificate of Appreciation from The Boy Scouts of America

- Served as a Board Member of McClain County Human Resource

- Served as an Executive Board Member of The Bridge, a shelter for battered women in Texas

About Moms Against Hunger

There are many ways Moms Against Hunger provides food because every mother wants to provide enough food for children to eat. We offer help and assistance to:

1. Impoverished nations, which receive food shipments that serve hospitals, schools, churches, communities, and refugee camps. Millions of packages of formulated rice meals are distributed in the developing world to provide essential nutrients, vitamins, minerals, and vital nourishment to the starving through Moms Against Hunger.

2. The "working poor," defined as those who work at jobs, but do not earn enough to provide adequate food for their families when an emergency happens.

3. Those who have lost their jobs due to economic reasons.

4. Homeless people who are without shelter and food.

5. Families in emergencies due to disasters such as hurricanes, fires, floods, tornados, and earthquakes.

Senior citizens who live on fixed incomes and need extra food sources.

Valuable, fortified rice meals are enriched with 51 percent vegetable protein, twenty-one minerals and vitamins, and nine dehydrated vegetables, all formulated by nutritionists to provide the perfect source of sustenance for a malnourished child.

Care is also taken to appeal to a broad variety of ethnic restrictions and tastes in every part of the globe. These meals include all nine of the essential amino acids necessary for a complete nutritionally complex meal. Rice or a bean-type food source cannot provide this balance alone. This food source is practical because it is complete in one bag, with five portions in each. It can be kept for long periods of time and only requires boiling water to convert it quickly into a complete food source for starving populations.

A shipping container can be packed with 250,000 meals. You, your organization, and Moms Against Hunger can ship one immediately to one of our worldwide distributions!

Moms Against Hunger ships water filtering systems to countries to protect, heal, and bring clean water to thousands of families in communities around the world.

African and South American nations as well as Mexico and Haiti have received Moms Against Hunger water systems in hospitals, schools, villages, and churches. This valuable system is portable and easy to carry in a backpack or gym bag. We welcome your assistance to provide pure drinking water to needy people around the world.

QUESTIONS AND ANSWERS

Moms Against Hunger is a 501(c)(3) not-for-profit relief organization providing food and supplies to needy families.

1. Does Moms Against Hunger receive government funding?

   No, we are a private organization and do not receive any government funding whatsoever.

2. Isn't the USA Food Stamp Program enough to feed people?

   No, when applying for food stamps, a family needs proof of employment such as the last two "pay stubs." Also income tax forms from the last year can be required—these totals are used to determine whether the family "qualifies" for food stamps. Thousands of families do not...*because this year's needs are determined by last year's income*. Often the chronically dependent receive the aid that the working poor cannot receive...simply because they are working and their wage earnings are just above the poverty level.

3. Can corporations donate?

   End-of-year gifts, overstock, and shelf pulls all can be useful in gifts-in-kind donations to the impoverished areas of the world. Together, corporate businesses work with Moms Against Hunger to meet the needs of orphanages, hospices, shelters, charity agencies, and Third World hospitals and medical clinics around the world. Does your corporation need help in this area? Contact us.

4. Are gifts to Moms Against Hunger tax deductible?

   We are a 501(c)(3) organization. All gifts are fully deductible.

5. When I make a gift to Moms Against Hunger, how much of the money goes to management and how much actually goes to the people?

   Our projects are structured so that all fundraising and management costs are covered by separate gifts and grants at this time, freeing the received donations to be used for the procurement and distribution of our programs around the world. Financial Stewardship of all resources is a primary concern at Moms Against Hunger.

6. Please tell me why people keep sending money to needs around the world and it never seems to get any better? Third World countries do not have infrastructures firmly in place:

No systematic form of farming education from government sources for farmers to learn such as soil types and responses, and systematic management of crops and land.

No equipment such as tractors, trailers, and other modern farm equipment to get food supplies from the farms to markets. Farming is still done *by hand* in most areas.

The road systems are often poorly managed and sometimes impassible—this creates another whole set of issues trying to get supplies to and from markets.

When crops are grown, many times the poor farmers do not have money for pest control—thus much of the food gets eaten or destroyed by animals, bugs, or fungus issues.

Droughts sometimes set in, causing further problems since nothing can grow without water.

If acts of war are in a country, people cannot go out in the fields.

Lands and farms are often seized by new governments and given to their supporters—who, in many cases, may have no experience or knowledge in agriculture, so good farm land goes fallow, and no crops are grown.

And the biggest issue of all these huge problems—people in poverty do not have money to buy food.

So you can readily see how food shortages around the world happen quickly. Each one of these subjects is immense, which is why caring and responsible people must give regularly to help vulnerable people in a variety of ways.

Moms Against Hunger works to provide a helping hand in an hour of need. To bring nourishing food and often a shoulder to lean on… just as a mother would do for her young in need.

We welcome you to be a monthly partner in helping Moms Against Hunger.

www.MomsAgainstHunger.org

Facebook: Moms Against Hunger

About NuCerity International

DREAMS TO REALITY

NuCerity International develops and distributes unique products that meet the demanding standards of the professional community as well as the needs of a shifting population. We produce first-to-market technologies that create new consumer categories in multi-billion dollar markets.

NuCerity's executive management team—all visionary entrepreneurs—has a history of successfully developing medical practices, launching strong retail brands, facilitating aggressive international expansion, and adapting distribution to meet the needs of divergent products in the global marketplace.

NuCerity International offers a comprehensive home-based business opportunity that can help you supplement your current income, replace it completely, or build a solid business foundation that can set the stage for lasting wealth. It is a conscious decision that NuCerity has chosen person-to-person marketing as the optimal channel to distribute its leading-edge products. We have a strong, experienced team of network marketing professionals and have designed a compensation plan that provides a clear, fair path to extraordinary income. We offer the support, training, and tools to help make your dreams a reality.

Because we understand that success is enhanced by a motivated, well-paid team, we will always value, respect, and protect the distributors' interests. Together, we will blaze new trails while helping inspire and empower people worldwide to look better, feel better, and live better.

NUCERITY'S VISION

Through daily commitment to our NuCerity team members, we will enable individuals and families globally to develop the greatness within themselves and create a future that allows them to retire with dignity and leave a legacy for future generations. We will inspire and empower those we touch. Together, we will live passionately, give radically, and create lives of impact, influence, success, and significance.

NUCERITY'S MISSION

We will provide proprietary, unique, and proven products, leading-edge business systems and tools, as well as unparalleled coaching, mentoring, and support for our global team members' journey toward self-empowerment, financial independence, and significance in their lives.

www.NuCerity.com

Facebook: NuCerity International

Personal Leadership Coaching

Dr. Gayla Holley has successfully coached clients, assisting each to grow the leader within. She has assisted clients to chart personal destinies and structure individual developmental growth and fulfillment since 1991. Through the three advanced personal systems entitled TimeWise, Executive Management Profile, and Capturing Significance, she coaches potential and active leaders. Dr. Gayla's personalized system has taken over twenty years to develop, and she currently coaches clients in individual and corporate leadership sessions each year. These inspiring systems include one-on-one coaching, weekly lessons, personal mentoring, and Webinar events directly from Dr. Gayla Holley. Her experience as an international keynote speaker and teacher gives her the knowledge base to help clients globally. She offers her Women in Leadership training several times a year for underprivileged women in impoverished areas.

TimeWise Coaching: Dr Gayla's specialized plan offers training lessons entitled, Control at the Wheel, Organized Chaos, and My Clock is Ticking, bringing efficient leadership into focus for the busy woman. This training will then serve as a tool for lifelong success in managing hectic work and family schedules.

Executive Management: A uniquely developed mind map for the administrative leader who finds the next rung on the ladder elusive. Dr. Gayla coaches the growing leader within, developing multiple facets by teaching lessons entitled Finding my Feet, The Chain Gang, and her new leadership Jungle Gym, a workplace authority on relationships.

Capture Significance: Charting the pathway of personal destiny will be revealed in this personal search with Dr. Gayla as your coach. Strategic sessions entitled Asleep at the Wheel, Dot to Dot, and The DreamBuilder's Guide will reveal the wonderful secrets of finding significance in success.

For a thirty-minute complimentary leadership consultation, please contact Dr. Gayla at **www.GrowingTheLeaderWithinYou.com**

Book Dr. Gayla Holley
To Speak at Your Next Event

When you are looking for a professional speaker for your next event, you will find Dr. Gayla Holley to be inspiring and entertaining as well as able to leave your audience with a renewed sense of purpose. She is one of the gifted speakers who can take you by the hand into her world and provide you with positive thoughts to enact change.

Dr. Gayla has been speaking professionally since the age of seventeen. She is as comfortable speaking to audiences of 20 as to 20,000. Dr. Gayla can communicate clear messages for your conference or seminars through interpreters. She understands that your audience is interested in real-life stories of achievement and inspirational growth. And her unforgettable style of warmth and humor touches the hearts of all who are privileged to hear her speak.

If you are looking for a speaker to help your group to achieve results, Dr. Gayla's extensive life experiences will leave your audiences wanting more. She speaks for many types of meetings, including business conferences, and social awareness, motivational skills, and women's events.

To learn whether she is available for your next meeting, contact her to schedule a complimentary pre-speech interview. You will love her the moment you meet!

drgayla@momsagaisthunger.org

Moms Against Hunger
2104 Underwood
LaPorte, TX 77571

Moms Against Hunger
P.O. Box 25
LaPorte, TX 77571